# AN UNIMAGINABLE
# J☼URNEY

## HOW PEPSI BEAT THE ODDS IN ROMANIA

# AVIAD MEITAR

ISBN: 1-4392-5050-2
ISBN-13: 9781439250501

Visit www.aviadmeitar.com to learn more about the book and the author

Visit www.booksurge.com to order additional copies.

# ACKNOWLEDGEMENTS

I wrote this book on behalf of the many people who took part in our "unimaginable journey". While it conveys my perspective of the journey, it attempts to tell the collective story of its participants and capture the essence of what we were able to create. Many of these people are mentioned by name; still more are there in spirit.

Every one of the participants played a unique role and helped make this journey so fascinating, enjoyable and ultimately successful.

I offer my sincere thanks to each one of you for your valuable contribution. Without your collective added value, this special story would not be there for me to write about.

There are a few people who deserve special mention: Jeff Fromm, who accompanied me on the very first trip to Romania and became a key player in the early years of the journey and thereafter; and Eli Davidai, who was the first manager of the Romanian venture and later came back to take the reigns and lead the business to its success. I consider myself very lucky to have had you as partners as well as close personal friends.

I would like to thank Kelly Jo Eldredge and Eric L. Mott for their significant contribution in their editorial role.

Last but not least, my family: my parents, my wife Ravit, my sons Yigal, Ayal and Yiftach - you are the heart and soul of every journey I take.

A.M.

# TABLE OF CONTENTS

# PROLOGUE

---

*You become a true circumnavigator only when you realize the futility of setting routes and stops.*

**—Reese Palley, *Unlikely Passages***

---

I would like to describe to you a journey. Not an ordinary trip one takes to the grocery store or the post office. This is an epic journey, a fantastic journey, an unimaginable journey. This journey seemed to start on an old and majestic, sluggish, lurching, creaking ship with billowing sails that were full at one moment and slack the next. Passengers came on board and disembarked often, impatient with its slow progress. But this journey was transformational for those who remained.

The ship altered its form before our weary eyes and became a winding caravan as our numbers increased and we lumbered across foreign territories unsure of where we were and where we were going. In a final burst of light, our transportation became a spaceship rocketing us into new dimensions and unlimited possibilities. What treasures this voyage held for those who followed it to the end.

I was one of the first travelers to set foot on that creaking ship. As I look back on the journey now, a smile crosses my face. Let me tell you about the unlikely crew that assembled in a haphazard manner to take a nearly impossible business opportunity and see it through to fruition. This was our journey.

"Wait! Do they serve drinks on this ship?"

"Why, yes."

"I'll take a Coke."

"Sorry, it will have to be Pepsi!"

# CHAPTER 1: EMBARKING

*Laugh at yourself, but don't ever aim your doubt at yourself. Be bold. When you embark for strange places, don't leave any of yourself safely on shore. Have the nerve to go into unexplored territory.*

**—Alan Alda**

It was the morning of July 25, 1990. I leaned back in a soft leather chair in my modest office on the fifth floor of an office building at the corner of bustling Fifth Avenue and Fifty-fourth Street in New York City. I was basking in the glow of new beginnings. I was young. I had a good job as a junior executive with Quadrant, the management arm of a private investment group called North American Resources. There was a vast ocean of opportunity before me professionally, and my personal life was also flourishing. I had married just six weeks earlier.

The phone rang, and the giant ship on which I did not even know I was a passenger lurched away from the docks.

"Could you come to my office?" It was Alan Quasha, the head of our investment group. I hopped up and made my way to his office, eager to hear about a possible new project. I had been with the group almost from its inception two years earlier, and during that period, I was privileged to take part in evaluating a long list of potential investments.

When I entered Alan's office, he handed me a very thin manila folder. "A few people from Kentucky approached us with the idea of setting up a Coca-Cola business in Romania," Alan said simply. "Take a look at that, and let me know what you think."

My eyes widened. So far, all of our investment opportunities had been in North America. I wasn't entirely sure I could easily locate Romania on a map. I took the folder and returned to my office through a fog of mental questions. However, they dissipated immediately when I received a second phone call. A close family member in Israel was about to undergo emergency surgery. I dropped everything and rushed to the airport.

Two weeks later, Saddam Hussein had invaded Kuwait and started an international affair that would have significant consequences on the world stage, I was not yet allowed to return to the United States because I was caught at the end of my work visa and forced to wait for its renewal. International storms were brewing around me, but I was suspended in a sort of neutral zone, temporarily prevented from moving forward or backward.

It was during that lull period that I received a call from a man who introduced himself as Dr. Qusai Al-Mahasneh. He was a member of the Kentucky group involved with the Coke venture I had only briefly heard about before rushing to Israel. Qusai didn't sound happy.

"You've got to help us," his edgy voice crackled over the international connection. "After months of moving this project along, Coke told us to take a hike. Do you know anyone in that organization that could get it back on track?"

I told him I would try to talk with someone. With the help of a family connection, I got in touch with a Coke executive and relayed the story. The answer was succinct and unwavering. "Coke will not work with the Kentucky group. They possess no expertise—neither in the beverage business nor in the international market."

There was not much room to negotiate with that statement, and I eventually returned to New York without a shred of good news for Qusai. The interesting new investment journey stalled before it ever left port.

I was disappointed by Coke's response, but I had reviewed only a small bit of information on the business opportunity at that point. Our firm had not yet made a commitment to the venture, so we were not particularly invested in its outcome. It was simply one of many interests that came and went without so much as a blip on our computer screens.

The members of the Kentucky group, however, were infuriated. They had spent months looking into the opportunity to launch Coke in Romania; they felt they knew the country, were convinced it offered enormous potential and were offended that Coca-Cola executives did not think they knew what they were doing. They turned their anger into action and marched right into the enemy's camp.

A few days after I returned to the United States, Qusai called again. "Never mind Coke," he told me. "We have approached Pepsi, and they're interested." There was no trace of the previous desperation in his voice. This time I detected a small, victorious glimmer of hope.

After they got the boot from Coke, the Kentucky group realized they had invested far too much time on this project to let it go to waste. There was only one other company that would have any interest in their acquired knowledge, Pepsi. So they contacted Coke's archrival by drafting a letter to Chris Sinclair, the head of Pepsi-Cola International (PCI).

Mr. Sinclair pushed the letter down the organization until it landed on a desk in Vienna. That desk belonged to Richard Norton, the area vice president in charge of Eastern Europe. This area was so unimportant to the PepsiCo organization at the time that it was stuck into a division headquartered in…Hong Kong. In a perfect example of synchronicity, the letter had slipped along the lines of the Pepsi-Cola International organizational chart and come to rest on Richard's desk at a most opportune moment.

Pepsi had actually been involved in Romania since 1967. The legendary founder of Pepsi-Cola, Don Kendall, developed his first barter deal scheme with Romania, in which Pepsi gave soft-drink syrup to a government agency in return for wine. The barter concept was so successful that he repeated it in 1972 with Russia in the famous Pepsi-Cola for ships and vodka agreement, endorsed by Nixon and Brezhnev.

From 1967 until the fall of communism at the end of 1989, Pepsi was produced in limited quantities in Romania and available exclusively to the inner political circle. The drastic political change in 1989 required Pepsi to alter their strategy. They suddenly needed a commercial partner to replace their defunct governmental one.

Pepsi executives searched frantically for a replacement and found a perfect ally in a company called Crescent. An executive at Crescent named Ioan Bucurescu had previously been responsible for approximately thirty-three food and beverage plants across the country, including the three plants that produced Pepsi. Ioan was intimately familiar with the production side of the business and had ample resources in Crescent. It was the perfect fit. Pepsi drafted a license agreement and planned to award it to Crescent, and then they hit rough waters.

Just days before the agreement was signed, various newspaper articles appeared that suggested Crescent was funded with old regime money. At the time that was tantamount to sleeping with the enemy. Pepsi needed to keep its reputation clean and therefore could not partner with such an entity. They were again left with a blank slate of candidates.

Opportunities for Pepsi in Romania stagnated. The wind had died down and there was no gust on the horizon to fill their sails—until

Richard got a hold of the letter from the Kentucky group. As he scanned its contents, he found that it contained signatures of Pepsi executives all the way up to the president of the company. He wasted no time and immediately invited the Kentucky group to travel to Vienna and give a presentation. Little did they know, they were the only candidates for the job.

Who made up this hopeful crew from Kentucky? Outwardly, it was an odd combination. The Kentucky group was comprised of three individuals who were thinly connected but strongly united in a common cause. Qusai was a Jordanian doctor who had studied medicine in Romania. Dennis Clare, the second member of the group, was a local attorney with an international clientele. The final member of the Kentucky group was Dr. Shelly Schiller, an ophthalmologist who was world renowned for a particular type of eye surgery. How did these men from different professions ever even cross paths? They played squash together.

In late December of 1989, the Romanian revolution culminated in the overthrow of its dictator, Nicolae Ceausescu. Three men in Kentucky watched the news and started to discuss business opportunities that would arise after the fall of communism in that region. Qusai knew Romania well and suggested they act immediately. What famous American brand could they bring to the changing country? Why, Coca-Cola, of course! Why not think big? A quick search revealed that Coke had no presence in Romania, and the Kentucky gang was off, speeding toward an untapped market at high velocity. They visited the country for the first time in January of 1990, just three weeks after the shooting stopped.

Several trips back and forth to Romania helped to clarify the situation for the Kentucky group. Their trips were organized as fact-finding missions. They immersed themselves in the country and learned everything they could about the culture, the politics, and the local beverage industry. They also came face-to-face with just how complicated it would be to make a foreign investment in Romania, but they were not dissuaded. They knew they could find a way to capture this elusive opportunity. What they needed was funds.

Shelly knew a man named Jeffrey Laikind, who was a seasoned investment banker in New York. They had played squash together as part of the U.S. team to the Maccabiah (Jewish Olympic) Games. He contacted Jeffrey to tell him their plan, and Jeffrey in turn contacted his business acquaintance, Alan, whom I reported to at Quadrant. The flimsy web of business opportunity made its way from Kentucky across the Atlantic to Romania and back to New York City as the threads tightened and strengthened and began to form a workable connection. The New York City thread may not have been as strong as the Kentucky group hoped at this early stage, but it was better than nothing. Alan gave a noncommittal answer that his firm *might* be interested, but the ever-optimistic Kentucky group took that as a green light and forged ahead.

The time had come for the Kentucky group to give their presentation in Vienna. By that time, they had accumulated a wealth of information on Romania, and they thought they might have an investor. It was not exactly a slam dunk, so they needed to be very convincing. Unfortunately, only one team member was available to make the trip to Vienna on the stated date. Shelly boarded a plane in late August of 1990 and faced Pepsi's Eastern Europe division solo.

Shelly came through for the Kentucky group and gave a compelling presentation. His message was that their group had acquired valuable knowledge on the country of Romania and the marketplace in that region, and that they had significant financial resources behind them.

"Are you prepared to commit five to ten or ten to twenty?" Richard asked at the conclusion of the presentation.

Shelly's response was quick and confident. "Ten to twenty."

Richard was impressed. He gave the Kentucky group the green light to proceed.

Shelly confided with me later that he had no idea whether Richard's question was referring to thousands or millions of dollars, but he was certain he could not afford to lose the opportunity by bidding low.

Shelly returned triumphantly to the Kentucky group, and Qusai immediately called me in New York.

"Where's the money?" he asked.

I was not exactly sure where to start in providing him with an answer.

"We were promised that your investment group would fund this project."

It was my turn to let the wind out of their sails momentarily. I explained that before we could even evaluate the business investment opportunity, we needed to see a business plan. They didn't have one.

The Kentucky group picked up the task and went back to work. They engaged a man by the name of Omar Assi, who became the next member of our unlikely crew. Omar was a personal assistant to the king of the United Arab Emirates, Sheik Maktoum, and an ex Coke executive. Over the next few months, I received drafts from Omar and the Kentucky group, and finally we were ready to meet.

In November of 1990, we scheduled two meetings. The first was between the Kentucky group and our investment fund. The second meeting was scheduled on the following day with a delegation from PCI. We had one day to come to an agreement between the Kentucky group and North American Resources before we faced the Pepsi team.

The Kentucky group started our first meeting with a proposal. They explained that since they had initiated the project and worked on it for a number of months to gather valuable information they would contribute their knowledge and retain a majority of the venture. The role of our investment group would be to fund the entire project, estimated by them to be around $25 million. North American Resources would receive a minority position in the venture in return.

The Kentucky group also proposed that Qusai manage the business while continuing his work in the field of medicine in Kentucky.

I asked Qusai about his credentials to manage a beverage business, and he was somewhat insulted.

"Just because I do not have an MBA does not mean I could not manage such a business," he retorted.

"Well," I responded, "I do have an MBA and, nevertheless, I do not profess to have the credentials to manage this business."

Alan took a moment and then countered with a proposal from our investment team. Our group was willing to fund the majority of the investment, but that value would be determined by us. We would receive a significant majority stake in the venture. The Kentucky group would be asked to make a modest investment toward which they could credit the time they spent to that point on developing the project, and they would receive a minority position. North American Resources would have managerial control of the project.

The Kentucky group asked for a brief intermission and adjourned to consult with Shelly's friend Jeffrey. A line had been drawn in the sand, and we waited to find out if we would continue this journey together.

Jeffrey gave the Kentucky group an honest answer. He told them our proposal was the best offer they were going to get from any investment group, and they should take it before it was too late. They returned and accepted our proposal, and we were ready to face the Pepsi delegation as a team.

On the following day, we waited with nervous anticipation in our New York office. Four members of the Pepsi delegation arrived: Josef Schmidt, an Austrian wine expert who was responsible for the Pepsi business in Romania, Bulgaria, and Albania; Walter Schilling, a German technical expert for Pepsi who cut short a business trip in the Far East to attend our meeting; Lou Aste, an attorney for Pepsi from Purchase, New York; and a midlevel executive from Pepsi headquarters.

The meeting did not go at all as we had planned. We prepared to lay out the credentials of our newly formed team and convince Pepsi that we were worthy partners, but Pepsi was barely interested. They were focused on convincing *us* that we should join them in this new Pepsi venture in Romania. Josef did such a terrific job of "selling" the Pepsi project that Alan agreed to send us on our first joint visit to Romania. I was given the task of organizing this next adventure. We were gaining crew members and picking up speed, as we gazed together across new seas of opportunity.

# CHAPTER 2:
# ROUGH WATERS ON THE
# MAIDEN VOYAGE

*A ship in port is safe,*
*but that is not what ships are built for.*

**—Grace Murray Hopper**

The excitement of initiating a new business proposition started to fade before we even made our first collaborative visit to Romania. I found myself defending the venture at the next executive meeting of our investment group. It was clear that most individuals in the room hated the idea. They pointed out that the mandate of North American Resources, as evidenced by its name, was *not* Romania, and that we possessed no expertise in the beverage industry. I insisted that this proposition was worth at least one visit to the country, and after much dispute, I finally received the green light from Alan.

Before embarking on our voyage, we started a preliminary due diligence process that would provide us with an ample supply of information for our trip to Romania. We interviewed a number of people and found out quickly that there was a wide variety of opinions on the country and its future, and most of them were on the negative side. It took some time to separate truth from fiction. One assistant to a U.S. congressman commented that Romania was the most illiterate country in Europe. That quote proved to be utter nonsense. We soon discovered that the one element that was valued in Romania, even under the old regime, was education.

The most valuable meeting we had was with Misu Negritoiu, the commercial attaché at the Romanian Embassy in New York. His advice was, "Do not spend your time in Romania meeting politicians. Instead, spend it on identifying the best potential business partners." This advice proved to be quite important along our journey.

The trip was planned for January 1991, and I encountered more problems as I tried to assemble a list of participants for the visit. The crisis in Kuwait was at a boiling point, and then the Gulf War started in full swing by January 15. It took more than a plane ticket to convince individuals to travel internationally during that time. At the very least, I needed one attorney from our affiliate law firm to join me, but none of the senior attorneys would accept my invitation. Many of them were handed a veto from their wives that included no opportunity for negotiation.

I finally approached Jeff Fromm. He was even younger than I and had very limited business-related experience. He had joined our affiliate law firm a few months earlier, leaving a much larger law firm. When I asked him why, he said that, among other reasons, he wanted more hands-on experience. I could certainly give him what he wanted. I made the offer, and Jeff accepted.

In late January 1991, Jeff and I left New York for Bucharest, via Vienna. The rest of our expedition team included Dennis and Shelly from the Kentucky group and Josef, the Austrian wine expert from

Pepsi. We took off with high hopes from our respective regions and landed together in a snowstorm. It was -6 Fahrenheit (-21 Celsius), and we peered out our cabin windows as the plane taxied through a white wall of snow toward an airport that looked like it had been hit by heavy artillery shells. Almost everything in sight appeared to be broken or shattered. Once we were in the terminal, a handful of working light bulbs created a dim, gray-grim atmosphere that seemed to herald impending doom. Our warm welcome also included an interminable delay in the airport as we wove our way through bureaucratic forms, questions, and searches before we were admitted into the country.

Finally, a welcoming smile greeted us as we exited the airport. It was Ioan Bucurescu. He and his partner, Costica Babiceanu, had left Crescent to become Pepsi consultants and they were instrumental in helping us organize our visit. Ioan would become our guide on this visit and every step of the journey from that point on. We had no idea how helpful Ioan would be in our adventure.

We had secured accommodations in the only semi-Western hotel in Bucharest, the majestic Intercontinental. Standing twenty-two stories high and looming over University Square, the hotel provided a convenient location in the center of the city. We arrived only a little over a year after the revolution. A significant portion of the events that changed this country had taken place right in University Square. One could still see bullet holes from the bloody event sprayed across the balconies facing the square. They were a constant reminder that change in Romania was not simply a business opportunity.

After we checked in, we were greeted by a young bellboy who, thankfully, spoke English fluently. He introduced himself as Robert and showed us to our rooms. When we asked him where he studied English, he claimed he learned by watching Robert Redford movies. As soon as he had us settled in our rooms, Robert offered to exchange U.S. dollars for the Romanian currency, leu (plural lei). The official exchange rate was 35 lei to the dollar, but Robert offered us

125 lei to the dollar. It was our first lesson in the difference between the official economy and the real economy.

I flicked on the television in my room as I unpacked and was happily surprised to see that the hotel offered CNN. It allowed me to follow what was happening in the Gulf War, which was of significant personal importance. Israel was under Scud missile attacks from Iraq, and my family was rushing daily to shelters and wearing gas masks as they waited out the bombing raids.

The next morning, we launched into action. First we visited Comaico, which was the location of one of three Pepsi plants in the country. It was situated about twelve miles outside of the city. Comaico was a complicated conglomerate of businesses. In addition to the Pepsi plant, it housed a dairy farm, slaughterhouses, a textile mill, greenhouses, and several other ventures. It was built as a showcase for the old regime, which is why Pepsi production was introduced into the jumble of industries at some point.

The plant was a disappointment. There was an ancient returnable glass line that had seen much better days, and the entire structure was situated in a dark and bitterly cold building. The heaters had been removed years earlier to conserve energy, and no one had yet bothered to put them back. A large number of people were required to operate the line, mostly because of the frequent technical maintenance needed to keep the old parts going.

As we left the plant, we were shown an end to an empty canal. Apparently, it was a pompous project Ceausescu devised to connect the Danube, which was flowing some thirty-five miles south of Bucharest, to the capital, so that he could claim the capital of Romania was also on the Danube. The revolution ended this crazy notion just a few miles short of completion, not before having wasted $1 billion of the poor nation's money.

Next, we visited the market, which was not bustling with commerce, but instead filled with empty government-owned stores. The weather was bone chilling, and I began to wonder what was worse, to walk around in the snow looking at dilapidated, closed storefronts in my thin leather shoes or to be driven around in locally produced Dacia cars—the Romanian version of a Renault 12. It seemed to be even colder inside those metal boxes with wheels.

Placing a call outside the country was another adventure altogether. It was before the cell phone era, and the only way to make an international call was to give the hotel receptionist the details and then wait in your room for two or three hours to get the connection. It was certainly not efficient and required that one be able to waste a chunk of time in the room hoping the phone would ring.

At the end of our trip, I think the overall feeling of the group looked exactly like the weather we experienced—gray, cold, sad, and disappointed. Every location we visited showed us exactly how forty-five years of communism and ruthless dictatorship took a significant toll on this ragged country. The conditions in which people lived and worked were appalling and very difficult for us to digest. The factories made it seem like we had stepped back in time to the age of the Industrial Revolution. When I think of what we experienced on that first trip, I wonder why we ever made a second visit.

Now I know why we went back. The reason was *hope*. We had the opportunity to bring hope to a community that was just starting to experience a market economy. If we could make this unique business proposition work and introduce an international brand like Pepsi into a significant market, it was most definitely worth a try.

There were twenty-three million people in that country—most of whom knew of the Pepsi brand but had never had the opportunity to taste the product. We had the prospect of reintroducing the brand to the entire country this time—not just the elite. We also had the power to help create jobs and business opportunities that would be essential ingredients in rebuilding the economy. We could help kindle the tiny free-market fire that was starting to burn in Romania.

Capitalism was far from a perfect model, and we would face many more storms as we continued on our journey, but hope burned within me that if we took this opportunity, there would be substantial rewards ahead for us and for the people of Romania.

# CHAPTER 3: ALL ABOARD

*A journey continues until it stops*
*A journey that stops is no longer a journey*
*A journey loses things on its way*
*A journey passes through things, things pass through it*
*When a journey is over, it loses itself to a place*
*When a journey remembers, it begins a journal*
*Which is a new journey about an older journey*
*A journey over time is different from a journey into time*
*An actual journey is into the future*
*A reflective journey is into the past . . .*

*A journey always begins in a place called Here*
*Pack your bags and imagine your journey*
*Unpack your bags and imagine your journey is done . . .*

*If you're afraid of a journey, don't buy shoes*

**—Mark Strand**

Our journey with Pepsi in Romania was fast becoming an intricate mix of all of Mark Strand's musings in the excerpt above from *Chicken, Shadow, Moon & More*. It never stopped or even slowed down a little; we certainly lost things along the way; we passed through many things; it took us into the future; and I should have bought warmer shoes.

I returned to New York disheartened but with the belief that the situation warranted learning a little more. I was asked to report on my visit at the next executive meeting and gave a balanced account of our findings. There was some pretty strong opposition in the room to taking this venture any further, but somehow I managed to keep Alan's support. That at least allowed me to continue on with the exploration phase of the project.

Jeff and I returned to Romania the following month. We explored more of Bucharest and initiated a discussion with Comaico about a possible joint venture. A "joint venture" was a popular term in those days that was loosely used to describe any form of cooperation between a foreign investor and a local partner. Our discussions were difficult every step of the way. The executives at the helm of that conglomerate were typical leftovers from the old guard. They spoke no English, had little or no exposure to Western business practices, and focused primarily on production. Sales, distribution, and certainly marketing were foreign concepts to these men. In addition, every single one of them was a chain smoker.

We came together in extremely long, tedious discussions in smoke-filled rooms, followed by Jeff staying up half the night to produce handwritten copies of any conclusions we had reached. He wrote the notes using a carbon copy so that we could review them with the heads of Comaico the following day. It was an era before laptops and easily accessible copiers and printers. The work was tiresome, and at that point, the fruits of our labor were not entirely evident.

Jeff and I returned to New York exhausted, but the opportunity was still alive. It might have been on life support at that point, but the heart was still beating. We were at a crossroads. The discovery period was over, and we needed to make a commitment to this venture. That meant we had to bring the proposition in front of the board of directors of North American Resources for their approval.

Alan informed me that the most I could ask the board to approve was a $5 million investment. So I took the business plan prepared by the Kentucky group, which called for a $25 million investment, and scaled it down. I took it down to the bare bones, and then I prepared a presentation for the board's quarterly meeting in March.

The day of the board meeting arrived, and our item was the least important on the agenda. Naturally, it was also the very last item to be discussed. There were six members on the North American Resources board: three representing Alan's family, and three representing his partner in the business, a Swiss public company called Richemont. By the time they were ready to hear my presentation, only three of six board members remained. They were Alan; Johann Rupert, the South African CEO of Richemont; and Eloy Michotte, a Belgian executive with Richemont.

I don't remember much of the presentation itself, but at the end of my talk, Johann asked me one question.

"If I were to give you personally a check for $5 million, what would you do with it?"

I answered without hesitation. "I would invest it in this venture."

"Then you have my support," he replied.

So with a vote of two to one, our venture got the support of the board. Eloy voted against it, because he claimed it was outside the clear mandate of the fund.

Johann did have one more thing to tell me before the meeting was adjourned. "I wish you every success with this venture. But succeed or fail, do not ever come back to the board for additional funds. None will be granted."

Johann explained that going against Coke was a losing battle, a bottomless barrel into which funds would be lost. That was why he had never before agreed to do business with Pepsi.

When North American Resources officially came on board that day, I knew I was facing a tremendous challenge. I would be taking on a fierce competitor with very little money comparatively—essentially, I would be fighting the enemy with bare hands. I was also putting my career on the line. Everything that I had achieved thus far with the group was placed on a scale, and the outcome of this new venture would tip the scales drastically in one way or another. As a Libra, I knew exactly how important it was for me to keep those scales from tipping in the wrong direction.

The business proposition was gaining momentum. We had board approval, and now we needed to get down to some serious work. Jeff and I went again to Romania in March and started to look for service providers. The first and most important providers we needed were a local attorney and an accounting firm.

We sought out the commercial attaché at the U.S. embassy, Kay Kuhlman, and she provided us with a list of references. We started with the attorneys and interviewed each using a list of questions to test their legal acumen. We thought we might be in trouble when we received responses like one from a university professor, who replied to a question with his own question.

"Do you want me to answer in the theoretical point of view or the practical one?"

We continued down the list of candidates and finally crossed paths with Ion Nestor. This man immediately struck us as someone who possessed good business judgment. Ion worked out of a modest office and called himself a "consultant" rather than an attorney. At that time, private attorneys in Romania were a new breed, and regulations stipulated they share a large portion of their fees with the bar association. After interviewing Ion, both Jeff and I felt he was a good match for our growing team.

Next, we discovered that Coopers and Lybrand had an office right in the Intercontinental Hotel where we were staying. We knocked on the door, and an attractive lady named Sylvia answered. She welcomed us into the office and introduced us to a man named Pierre Vigroux, who was the head of the local branch. Pierre was a Frenchman who sounded exactly like Inspector Clouseau. We immediately hit it off.

Jeff and I were starting to feel pretty good. We had secured a local attorney and an accounting firm. Things were falling into place. Full of optimism, we decided to venture outside of Bucharest for the first time. We traveled to the city of Constanta on the Black Sea. Little did we know, it was not an ideal season to travel to this harbor city. Its busy season did not start until June, and hotels were not prepared to cater to winter guests. Rooms offered minimal heat, and I found myself wearing multiple layers of clothes to bed and collecting all the blankets I could find in my room.

In Constanta, we visited our second Pepsi plant in Romania, Munca Ovidiu, named after the Roman poet who was exiled to that area, the most remote province of the old Roman Empire. This was in fact the first of the Pepsi plants, opened in 1967. It was historically interesting, as we were able to take a look at the first bottle of Pepsi ever produced in Romania—or the entire communist block for that matter. It was gold plated and displayed as an ornament to success in the factory. Unfortunately, the plant had not changed much since 1967. It was in desperate need of updated technology, and we learned that the quality of product it produced was negatively affected by the condition of the machinery in the plant. The poor condition of the plant would play a significant role in our geographic setup in the Black Sea region in the coming years.

We returned to New York with a much stronger sense of purpose. Our ancient ship seemed to be finding its course. We had picked up valuable crew members, and we all looked to the horizon to catch a glimpse of what lay ahead. Our adventure had begun in earnest, and there was little chance of turning back for those of us who had agreed to sign on.

# CHAPTER 4: SETTING SAIL

*Twenty years from now you will be more disappointed by the things that you didn't do than by the ones that you did do. So throw off the bowlines. Sail away from the safe harbor. Catch the trade winds in your sails. Explore. Dream. Discover.*

**—Mark Twain**

At this point, our course was chosen, and we seemed to be gaining momentum on the open seas of opportunity. We received the first draft of a document called the Exclusive Bottling Appointment (EBA) from Pepsi. It was basically the license agreement between PepsiCo and a bottler, and it governed the entire relationship. The EBA was fondly referred to as "the Bible" within Pepsi, because not only did it serve as the rule book for every aspect of the relationship, but a prospective bottler was expected to sign on the dotted line at the end without asking for many changes.

Jeff did not know about that expectation and innocently asked if he could suggest a few changes. The answer was a surprising yes. Pepsi said he was welcome to create a new draft of the document if he so desired. This unusual response was probably the result of two things: the legal department at Pepsi International already had too many projects on its plate, and no one at Pepsi International thought Romania would become a significant project. So the door was open for Jeff to rewrite the Bible, and he did.

We looked closely at every clause in the EBA and made numerous changes. The result was a much more balanced document that would prove to be an invaluable tool over the coming years. We were very lucky to slip through this potentially rocky passage and integrate important changes without getting caught in the endless process of legal haggling.

Our next trip to Romania in April demonstrated just how exciting it was to become a new member of the Pepsi tribe. We were welcomed with open arms. Jeff and I stopped in Vienna, which was our usual connection to Romania, but this time we stayed for a few days to attend a grand event called "The Pepsi-Cola International Area VP Award." This ritual was left over from the communist era and provided a legitimate business excuse for bottlers to travel abroad and attend a festive occasion. One manager from each Eastern European country was selected and invited to attend the lavish affair.

Pepsi-Cola excelled at sponsoring events to honor their bottlers across the globe. The experience included a guided tour of Vienna, a number of sumptuous meals, and an evening cruise on the Danube. It culminated in a formal dinner at which special awards were given to the select bottlers. Jeff and I were each invited to bring a guest, and our inclusion signaled to us that we were now part of the Pepsi family. It was incredibly reassuring to feel so welcomed and supported.

After the award ceremony, we continued on to Romania in style. Pepsi chartered an executive jet to transport Josef, Walter, Ioan, Costica, Jeff, and me on our journey. Just as we were starting to feel a little pompous about our newly acquired status within the ranks of Pepsi, we realized that it was simply the more economical choice. We were scheduled to visit a number of locations around the country, and flying the regular commercial route would have been a logistical nightmare. Domestic flights in Romania were set up like spokes on a wheel. They only went from Bucharest to the destination city and back. With an executive jet, we were able to save quite a bit of time by flying directly from one city to the next.

Our first destination was Arad, a town in the western part of Romania close to the Hungarian border. We received a touching welcome from local children wearing regional costumes. They handed us flowers and sang joyful traditional songs that contained a vibrant local flavor. This was followed by a guided tour of the city and the market.

Our next stop was Suceava in the far northeastern part of the country, close to Romania's border with the Ukraine. There we were greeted by a group of dancers. They performed rousing traditional dances and invited us to join them. It was a wonderful experience to soak up the culture of the Romanian people in various parts of the country. Everywhere we traveled, we observed people who were proud of their heritage and enjoyed sharing their rich traditions with visitors.

We toured the outskirts of Suceava to see one of many monasteries in the region that was famous for its glass window paintings. The artistry was extraordinary. When we returned to the city, we were met with yet another surprise. We were invited as guests of the regional government office to stay at Ceausescu's villa, which had been turned into an exclusive inn after the revolution. Ceausescu had many such villas around the country. We could hardly believe our eyes as we walked into the stately mansion with wood and marble floors, high ceilings, and elaborate decorations.

The room assignments were handed out: Walter got Ceausescu's room; Jeff was given Elena's, the late dictator's overambitious wife, who many claimed was responsible for his extreme policies in the final years of his rule. As a slightly morbid inside joke, every bedroom contained a diary opened to December 21, 1989. Ceausescu and his wife were captured on that date and later executed.

Our crew was served a delicious meal in the spacious dining room, and after dinner we went bowling in a semiautomatic bowling alley that had been installed in the villa. We returned to our rooms satiated with hospitality. The only downside was that the heating system was not sufficient to properly heat the large place. We awoke the next morning to learn that our experience came with a price tag. Each Romanian citizen in our group was charged the equivalent of $5 in local currency. Each foreign member of the group was charged $125 in hard currency! We learned an important lesson in receiving local "favors."

Aside from the lavish accommodations and entertainment, we had important business in both Arad and Suceava. Pepsi chose the sites for our trip, because they were interested in adding returnable bottling lines in those locations to expand the manufacturing landscape. The purpose of our visit was to advance those plans.

At the conclusion of our tour of Suceava, we took off for Bucharest, where the Pepsi group continued on to Vienna, and Jeff and I stayed for a few days to further our efforts to establish a local presence.

Our focus was to continue negotiations with Comaico on a possible joint venture. It felt much more like a tango than a negotiation process. For every two steps forward, we took one step back. The plan on the table was for us to take an interest in the entire conglomerate. We wanted a solid controlling position, but the issue at hand was how to evaluate the company's asset base.

Jeff and I introduced the concept of a 70-30 ownership split in our favor early in the discussions. It was now a matter of supporting that concept by attaching a certain value to the company as it stood and comparing that to the contribution our side was willing to make. We were stymied by the fact that the management of Comaico was not well versed in the customary universal valuation methods.

Another equally important task was our discussions with a government agency called the Romanian Agency for Development. This agency was charged with approving every foreign investment in Romania. They were assigned the task of making sure the relative valuations were fair.

The senior executives of the Romanian Agency for Development were mostly old bureaucrats, who appeared to be supportive of foreign investors but had no sense of urgency in advancing matters. During a phone conversation with one of these VPs, the line was abruptly cut off. I thought there must have been a technical problem with the phone line, which was a frequent occurrence in Bucharest. So I rushed to their office to resume our conversation. I arrived to find the VP sitting casually at his desk reviewing another matter. It was clear that he had simply hung up on me to deal with a different issue.

Jeff and I realized on this trip that it was becoming increasingly important for us to have someone locally who could maintain momentum on various matters in between our visits. In another synchronistic episode of timing and opportunity, we were led to Peter Tagge. He was an American and a Harvard MBA who had been living in Romania for some time—and he was available to work for us. We negotiated a contract that included accommodations in the apartments section of the Bucharest Hotel to be used as a makeshift office. We had hired our first local employee, thus planting our corporate flag in Romania!

This trip had already been full of colorful characters and scenes, but the most interesting chapter was yet to be revealed. I received a call in my hotel room from someone who introduced himself as Reese Palley. He didn't reveal much, other than the fact that he was down in the hotel lobby and wanted to meet with me.

"I have a funny hat with lots of pins attached to it. You will have no problem recognizing me."

Curiosity got the best of me, and down to the lobby I went. Mr. Palley did not lie. He was certainly easily recognizable—an elderly American with a funny tourist hat. I found out that Reese happened to be cruising the Black Sea at the time of the revolution, part of a circumnavigation trip he was taking on a small yacht, and decided to stay and open the first advertising agency in the country. When he heard about our intentions to become the Pepsi bottler in that region, he decided to make us his pet project.

I liked Reese immediately. From our very first meeting he bubbled over with interesting ideas for Pepsi advertising campaigns. I told him there was only one problem: we were not yet the Pepsi bottler and had not established a business presence. It was far too early to discuss advertising. My cautionary words did not deter Reese in the least. He visited us every time we traveled to Romania from then on, armed with creative advertising ideas and begging us to allow him to get started.

On our way back to New York, Jeff and I stopped in Vienna once again. This time, in addition to meeting with the usual Pepsi team, we met with Les Hamm, the division president. He had flown in from headquarters in Hong Kong specifically to meet us. Evidently, Mr. Hamm needed to check us out in person before officially signing us on as a Pepsi bottler. Over decadent pieces of Sacher torte in the hotel that made the cake famous, we passed the test.

Jeff and I were jubilant when we returned to the United States, and my excitement multiplied when I learned that I had not one but two important projects underway. My wife was pregnant with our first child.

There was much work to be done. We had no time to celebrate our victories. It was time to look for a manager to run the business we were forming. We needed an able captain for our ship, and it had to be someone from outside the country. We hired a United States-based executive search firm through our local contacts and described to the firm our needs and the business environment before sending them on their mission. We also met with an Austrian search firm that claimed to have extensive regional experience and a large pool of executives from which to choose. We presented them with a mandate to look for an executive in Europe. With the help of these two reputed search firms, we felt confident that we would end up with a strong list of candidates.

In addition, we were moving ahead on the EBA with Pepsi. They complained a little that we were asking for too many changes to the Bible, but they were cooperative in the end. Pepsi agreed to allow us to add our proposed language that made the relationship more balanced.

As an example, the original EBA gave Pepsi the power to act capriciously and still remain well within its rights. We added the word "reasonable" in certain paragraphs to provide us with additional leverage and security. Once we had done everything it took to build a Pepsi business, we did not want to lose our license without very good cause and time to cure our faults.

Alan also insisted that we insert a "most favored nation" clause. This clause meant that we would be assured by Pepsi that on key elements of the deal—most importantly the price of concentrate—no one would get a better deal than we would. Romania was at the very bottom of the world economy at that time, and we felt this clause would be only fair. Pepsi ultimately agreed to it.

At the end of May, we geared up for our next monthly trip to Romania. On route to Bucharest, I learned that Chris Sinclair, PepsiCo International's president, had signed our EBA at their headquarters in New York. It was May 28, 1991. I added my signature, and we officially became the exclusive Pepsi-Cola bottler for the country of Romania. I tasted success, but the journey had just begun.

# CHAPTER 5: LIVING BY VIKING LAWS

*__Be brave and aggressive.__*
*Be direct.*
*Grab all opportunities.*
*Use varying methods of attack.*
*Be versatile and agile.*
*Attack one target at a time.*
*Don't plan everything in detail.*
*Use top quality weapons.*

*__Be prepared.__*
*Keep in shape.*
*Find good battle comrades.*
*Agree on important points.*
*Choose one chief.*

*__Be a good merchant.__*
*Find out what the market needs.*
*Don't promise what you can't keep.*
*Don't demand overpayment.*
*Arrange things so that you can return.*

*__Keep the camp in order.__*
*Keep things tidy and organized.*
*Arrange enjoyable activities which strengthen the group.*
*Make sure everybody does useful work.*
*Consult all members of the group for advice.*

**—The Viking Laws**

O ne thousand years ago, Nordic seamen roamed the oceans in their longboats, conquering nations and launching Pepsi franchises wherever they went. Not really. But on a recent trip to Scandinavia, I became fascinated with Viking culture and discovered our Pepsi team had a lot in common with those long-ago sailing men bravely exploring uncharted waters. During my trip, I found a poster listing ancient Viking laws—laws that apply beautifully to running a successful business in modern times. That poster has hung on my office wall ever since.

While we were struggling to set up our business in Romania, we didn't know how many of the Viking laws we could have...or *should* have applied to our day-to-day business decisions. The histories and cultures of countries may vary, but the rules of success are universal.

*Attack one target at a time.* The entire time we worked to establish Pepsi in Romania, we were aware of one very dangerous and elusive enemy—Coke. We had no idea what they were planning for this new market, and we had a constant feeling of looking over our shoulder and wondering what our greatest competitor was up to. We always kept in the forefront of our minds the fact that Coke was our one real target. We wanted to blow them out of the water before they had a chance to settle in to this new area of interest.

We found our first opportunity for attack in the form of a gift. PCI gave us a large illuminated Pepsi-Cola sign as a welcome-to-the-family present when we signed our bottling agreement. Where could we place this logo in Bucharest for all to see?

We identified a beautiful building right in University Square, and with the help of Ioan, we found two young business people who claimed to have the rights to place the sign at that location. After a short period of negotiation, we agreed to a fee and gave them the mandate to obtain the necessary approval and place the sign.

On our next visit, we grinned as we entered University Square. Our sign glowed atop that building for all to see. It was as if we had planted our flag in the market and dared Coke to enter our territory. The sign quickly became a famous symbol in Bucharest. Whenever there was an important event in Romania, such as the election of a new president, the homecoming of the national soccer team, or other national event, the festivities took place in University Square. National televisions stations gave us great exposure during every event, as the Pepsi logo shone brilliantly over each occasion.

*Arrange enjoyable activities which strengthen the group.* One aspect of our visits to Romania in those days that was truly lacking was variety of food. Restaurants that served Western-style food were nonexistent, and we ended up eating most of our meals at the Intercontinental Hotel. Soon we had sampled every single item on the menus of the two restaurants at the hotel, we knew most of the waiters, and we could sing along with the entire repertoire of the piano player.

Jeff and I were starved for something new, and we started asking around for restaurant recommendations in Bucharest. One well-meaning local suggested we try an eating establishment that had been around for 150 years. It sounded promising, so we checked it out. We walked tentatively into this restaurant that had survived communism, dictators, and revolutions, and it looked like it had seen better days. We took our chances and ordered lunch. The dining experience on the whole was quite terrible. The meat was inedible, even with the help of special knives provided by the proprietor. And after we made a halfhearted effort at pretending to enjoy our dining experience, we received two bills: one for the food in local currency, and the other for our soft drinks in U.S. dollars. We returned, defeated, to our hotel for the next meal.

*Consult all members of the group for advice.* Sylvia, the office manager at our accounting firm, also provided restaurant suggestions. She and her husband, Gigi, invited us to the only Chinese restaurant in Bucharest. We were quite excited about the prospect of an exotic new menu. The place looked the part with traditional Chinese decorations donning the walls and tables. The menu contained semi-

Chinese-looking dishes, but something was not quite authentic. When we requested chopsticks, we were told that all Chinese "equipment" departed with the staff. Evidently, they were called back to China soon after the revolution. That explained the quasi-Chinese fare that was served.

Our quest for new culinary experiences became a bit of a joke, but it ultimately strengthened our small group through humor, if not culinary satisfaction.

Our new office space also left something to be desired. We housed Peter, our first local employee, in the long-term wing of the Bucharest Hotel, and his accommodations included room for our first makeshift office—a very small, cramped office that probably had a capacity of three individuals. Lucky for us, it was usually inhabited by only one man.

Unfortunately, the new office space also provided us with no easy way to communicate with our single staff member. Most of the time, when we tried to call from the United States, we could not get through. Either the phone system would falter, or the operator at the hotel would just hang up on us. Complaining produced zero results. The concept of service was relatively unknown there.

Our visits at this time focused on solidifying a relationship with Comaico. It was extremely difficult to coax the management of this organization to take action. In an attempt to get something moving, we offered to import Pepsi cans and allow the company to sell the product to their customers. We offered 10 percent of the profit, and they seemed very satisfied with that prospect. We were flabbergasted to realize partway through our talks that the executives at Comaico thought we meant 10 percent of the selling price. That would have been more than 100 percent of the expected profit! It took a bit of time to straighten out that misunderstanding, but what was really astonishing to us was that senior management completely confused turnover with profit. They had clearly never before focused on profitability.

We also tried to convince the Comaico executives to increase the price of their 250 ml returnable bottle. At the time, they were selling it for a measly 6 lei, or about 17 cents at the official exchange rate. Management at Comaico staunchly believed that sales would drop off if they raised the price. That notion was ridiculous considering production capacity was so low in all three Pepsi plants at the time that it was impossible for them to keep up with demand. We managed to convince the leaders at Comaico to increase their price, but only very slowly. They continued to sell out of everything they were able to produce.

*Find good battle comrades.* Progress on forming the joint venture was slow at best. Each time we thought we were making progress, a new obstacle blocked our path. First, the general manager with whom we were negotiating passed away suddenly. His successor had a different perspective and brought up a whole slew of new issues. Once we worked through the new issues and thought we had reached a general agreement, we arrived in Bucharest to find the Ministry of Agriculture had replaced the entire management team at Comaico. Evidently, this was a well-established trick. If the government agency responsible for a business was unhappy with an agreement they were reaching with a foreign partner, they "shuffled the cards." A change in management meant they could claim the agreement was not valid.

We needed to bolster our negotiating team, so we beefed up our crew with a very senior New York attorney on the next visit. Negotiations continued, and at some point, we were haggling over the definition of "force majeure." Our savvy new ally and counsel suggested including in the definition "any day during which trade on the New York Stock Exchange is halted." We were met with blank expressions. Our counterparts had no clue what that meant and why it should be considered as part of the definition. It was a fine lesson in cultural differences.

While the tug-of-war ensued over a joint venture, we started to look at bottling production equipment that would upgrade our facility of choice once a deal was done. PepsiCo's technical staff pointed us to where secondhand equipment was available. On June 25 I visited a Pepsi plant in Detroit to look for such equipment, and I was accompanied by a Pepsi employee from Slovenia. I remember that date vividly, because it was the day Slovenia declared independence from Yugoslavia. My trip-mate was naturally nervous about potential ramifications. As it turned out, Slovenia's mission was much more successful than ours. There were about ten days of token military action, and then Slovenia was recognized as a sovereign country. We continued to look for a satisfactory conclusion on other fronts.

*Choose one chief.* It was now late June, and while we were at least moving forward on a number of fronts, we were quite anxious about the total lack of progress in one area: finding a chief. The two executive search firms we hired had not produced a single viable candidate in three months of exploration. We were quite frustrated, especially since we were paying good money to two excellent firms to find this needle in a haystack. We needed a manager, and the time was now.

In my despair, I called my uncle, who was a very seasoned businessman.

"Why don't you look here in Israel?" he asked.

He referred me to a local executive search firm, and within ten days, they had rounded up six credible candidates. Right after Fourth of July weekend, Jeff and I flew to Israel to interview them. We narrowed the list down to two individuals, Eli Davidai and Amiram Amit. The next logical step in the interview process would be for them to meet the rest of our team and tour their potential new workplace. It would have been an easy task to arrange in a typical business environment but, so far, our venture was far from typical.

In a somewhat unorthodox decision, we decided to fly both candidates to Romania at the same time so that they could see the business environment firsthand and meet some of their potential colleagues.

Then, we flew them to New York to meet our senior management team and finalize the interview process. In execution, the final round of interviews was complex. The two competitors for the position graciously agreed to travel together to aid us in our decision-making process, and it was not an easy choice. Both men were well qualified and possessed numerous strengths. In the end, I made the final decision and chose Eli Davidai to manage our beverage business in formation. In retrospect, this was a key decision that had significant impact on the business venture and signaled the beginning of a long, close, and unique relationship. We had our chief.

We immediately needed a legal entity to hold the emerging activity in Romania. On July 12, almost a year after I first learned of this business opportunity, we registered a company in the British Virgin Islands. The Kentucky group had chosen the name Amroq for their company, formed from **AM**erican-**RO**manian-**Q**uadrant. We wanted to combine the names of the two principal companies to create our new legal entity. Finally, we selected Quadrant-Amroq Bottling Company Limited. That was quite a mouthful, and soon everyone started to refer to the company by its acronym, QABCL.

Unfortunately, with two issues solved, another immediately surfaced. We arrived in Bucharest for our next visit, and Ioan greeted us as usual at the airport. This time he did not look as welcoming. He handed us a pile of papers and told us Peter had resigned with no explanation. In fact, he never showed his face at the Bucharest Hotel again. Now there was no one to maintain momentum in between our visits. We also admitted during this visit that discussions with Comaico were going nowhere. We had wandered down the wrong road and sat at a dead end, but failure was not an option. We planned our next strategy. We needed new alternatives.

*Grab all opportunities.* Reese showed up again, armed with a host of advertising ideas to lighten our moods. This time, one of his brainstorms was just too good to pass up. In August, the United States would face Romania in their first ever football (soccer) match. It would take place in Brasov, a resort town about three hours north of Bucharest.

Reese came up with the following idea: we would fly Ambassador Green, the American ambassador and a close friend of President George Bush, Sr., to the venue by helicopter. The ambassador would emerge from the helicopter at midfield wearing a Pepsi cap and then would kick the first ball. The event would be aired on Romanian national TV, which was the only channel available locally, so ratings would be quite high. Evidently, the entire affair would cost us only $10,000. I gave Reese the green light, so to speak, and he pulled it off with stunning success. It was Pepsi's first advertising effort in Romania.

Reese gave us momentum to continue pushing forward, and our next step was to find a replacement for Peter. That person emerged in the form of a towering ex-Romanian who had lived in the United States for a number of years. His name was Vladimir Chirileanu, and he was quite excited to return to his home country as a representative of a well-known American company. Vladimir quickly situated himself in Bucharest, and we relaxed in the knowledge that we once again had someone on the ground to take care of business in between our visits.

We should not have been so quick to drop our guard. Vlad was very active in the beginning of his term, but he turned out to be another shooting star on our journey. Within a few months, he returned to the United States on a stretcher, after claiming to have hurt his back avoiding being hit by a car. Vlad started to collect on our disability insurance, and we never saw him again.

On our August trip to Romania, we officially abandoned our talks with Comaico and turned our attention to Flora. This was the third Pepsi plant in Romania, and we had previously ignored it because of its small size. Flora was located right in the middle of Bucharest. Unlike the numerous industries at Comaico, Flora only had three activities going on. It produced Pepsi, it produced unbranded local soft drinks and it produced canned goods.

The Pepsi line at Flora was ancient and in very similar condition to the one at Comaico. Their local soft drink production line was even worse. And then there was the canning line! That high-tech operation consisted of a bunch of women shoving peas and other vegetables into glass containers with their bare hands.

We prepared ourselves for the worst and met with the general manager, Mr. Greceanu and his team. Suddenly, it was as if bright sunlight broke through the storm clouds that loomed above us. Mr. Greceanu was receptive. He actually saw in us a unique opportunity to take his fledgling business to new heights by turning it into a joint venture with a well-capitalized international company. Our discussions moved swiftly, and in two short rounds of discussions we arrived at an agreement on forming the joint venture.

Flora would contribute its entire assets base, which included nearly ten acres of land on which the plant stood. We would contribute working capital and new production equipment. To demonstrate our commitment to the deal, we placed a new filler in Flora's old Pepsi production line before the agreement was signed. This one bit of equipment improved production capacity, but more importantly, it helped seal the deal.

There was only one small glitch in the joint venture agreement process with Flora. When I introduced the equity split, I changed the figures of 70 percent and 30 percent that we had presented to Comaico to 75 percent and 25 percent in our favor. This was because Flora was a much smaller entity and so was their asset base to be contributed to the joint venture. Ioan was translating, and he accidentally repeated the "old" figures. I caught on to his slip only later in discussions, and our counterparts felt robbed of 5 percent when it was sorted out. We managed to overcome the issue, and the official contract signing was scheduled for early October.

The momentous day came on October 11 and, unfortunately, I was unable to attend. Jeff represented us by himself. The main task was for both parties to sign multiple copies of the agreement, and a signature was required on each and every page. Jeff and Mr. Greceanu must have attached their signatures to some three hundred pages that afternoon, and the entire event was videotaped. They kept smiling for the camera, even though their hands were cramping up; in the end, we had a vehicle to carry out our business. Its name was Sitaco.

We had secured the Pepsi license a few months earlier, and now we had the joint venture in place. We were inching closer to the start of our business, and it was time to plan for that eventuality. First, we had to close the contract with Eli. He had chosen a few executives to bring with him to form his management team, and we had a number of issues to work out in addition to compensation and benefits. Some of those issues were more unusual than others, due to our business location. For instance, we inserted a clause that if there were food shortages in Romania, we would commit to flying fresh produce to our employees.

The contracts were finalized, and next we needed to find proper housing for Eli and his family. We contracted a local agency and started to look around. Most homes were unsuitable, and we were beginning to get a little worried about finding something appropriate. Then, we came across a villa in a quiet neighborhood where quite a few embassies were housed. It belonged to the family of Peter Grosa, the first communist prime minister of Romania. After the fall of communism, the family managed to secure ownership of the villa and they rented out a majority of the space in exchange for badly needed income. We immediately agreed to a two-year rental contract.

Another detail that seemed to elude us was finding a driver for Eli. It was clear he would need to cover a great deal of territory as part of the job. One day I was driving around with Ioan, and he stopped the car abruptly in the middle of the street.

"I found your driver," he said with a smile.

Right there on the side of the road stood a short, jolly person named Mihai. He had been Ioan's driver in his old government job. Ioan convinced the little man to come work for us within minutes, and we checked manager's driver off the to-do list. What an important asset Mihai would prove to be.

Eli joined us on our next visit in late October. Among other things on our agenda, we visited Topoloveni, a sleepy little town about an hour and a half from Bucharest by car. There was a bottling company there that we wanted consider for our manufacturing base of operation in the country. Eli began learning Romanian only a couple of weeks prior to this trip, but he jumped right into the fray and started speaking Romanian with the people we encountered on this journey. He was very well received. Our contacts clearly appreciated Eli making an effort to connect with them in their own language. We could already see we made a wise choice in hiring this leader.

PCI knew we had limited experience in the beverage industry. Rather than dismissing our ignorance, they supported us by connecting us with people who would complement our resources. One such person was Anday Kragaris. Andy was originally from Greece and had been involved with Pepsi largely in the "on premise" sector, which meant in restaurants, cafes, bars, and the like. He was Pepsi's licensee in that sector in Montreal, Canada.

That one connection led to a whole other network. Andy was neighbors with Joseph Pandelli, whose father had been involved with business in Romania for over thirty years. The Pandellis were Syrians, and their business was trade between Syria and Romania. Executives at PCI thought we should consider partnering with Andy and the Pandellis in the emerging on-premise segment of the beverage business. Jeff and I felt the idea was certainly worth further exploration, so we flew to Montreal, met with Andy and Josef, and strengthened that connection.

On our next visit to Bucharest, we met the patriarch of the Pandelli family. The elder Pandelli was sharp. He suspected immediately that I was from the Mediterranean. He sized me up and then asked if I was Moroccan. I replied that I was Israeli, and he was quite shocked. I also told him that both my wife and brother-in-law were of Syrian Jewish decent.

"What is their name? Nechmad?", Pandelli Sr. questioned.

It was my turn to be shocked. The surname of my brother-in-law was in fact Nechmad. This Syrian Arab, whom I met for the first time in Romania, knew a branch of my immediate family very well. The cliché about it being a small world proved itself yet again in this unique and unlikely connection. The Pandelli family invited us to a homemade Syrian meal, which they served in the main dining room of the Intercontinental Hotel. Finally, we had an excellent diversion from our uninspired restaurant choices in Romania.

At the end of the meal, the Pandellis asked us for our dessert orders. I responded that their exquisite Mediterranean meal called for baklava as dessert. They were disappointed that they weren't able to offer it that evening, but they promised to arrange for some on our next visit. When I arrived on my next trip, I had six boxes of varieties of the best baklava I have ever tasted waiting for me. It came straight from the Daud Brothers in Damascus.

*Use varying methods of attack.* It had become routine for Reese to hunt us down with a new presentation of advertising ideas every time we visited Bucharest. At this point, I was more confident in the likelihood of there actually being a Pepsi business in Romania, so I was receptive to his inspirations. We decided to act on two of his proposals in the latter part of the year.

The first method of attack was to advertise on buses. Reese secured an exclusive deal with a local bus company. It cost us $75 per bus per month. Soon, we started seeing Pepsi ads pop up on buses all over Bucharest. Our ads caught the public eye, because that type of advertising had never been done before in Romania.

Our second angle of attack was in the cinemas. When Reese came to us with a deal of $1 per minute of advertising, we thought he was joking. The cinemas were filled to capacity, even though they showed mostly second-rate movies. We had an opportunity to get the Pepsi brand in front of large groups of people for peanuts. The ads ran for a number of months, and they were not removed until our marketing team decided to discontinue them.

*Use top quality weapons.* It was time to choose our weapons. We had committed to providing equipment in the joint venture with Flora, and we needed to get to work on finding it. PCI combed its international connections and sent me to Germany with a PepsiCo technical team to inspect a secondhand PET, or polyethylene, line that handled nonreturnable plastic bottles rather than returnable glass containers. That inspection yielded good results, and we agreed on a turnkey project. The dealer would finish an overhaul on the line, deliver it to our facility in Bucharest, and install it for us. We gave a down payment and agreed on a timeframe for the project before leaving Germany.

The next important weapon we needed to secure was a carbon dioxide production plant. $CO_2$ is a key ingredient in any carbonated beverage, and supply in the Bucharest area was limited. Our new bottling line required quite a bit more than the current supply. Again, PCI put its vast resources to use and provided us with the name of a Danish company. It took little time for us to make a commitment to that company and secure an adequate supply of $CO_2$.

Toward the end of the year, PepsiCo decided to cancel its license with Munca Ovidiu, the plant in Constanta that was the first Pepsi production plant in all of Eastern Europe. The decision was justified after numerous warnings about quality issues at the plant, but we regretted it nevertheless. Our command of the Pepsi business in Romania was imminent, and if PepsiCo had waited for us to correct the quality issues there, we could have had one more production line available to us.

It was extremely important for us strategically to place operations throughout the country in the early stages. The only packaging used at that time was a returnable glass bottle, which meant that each bottle had to travel twice—from the plant to the marketplace and then back to the plant. A bottling plant therefore was able to serve a perimeter of only around one hundred miles, and cutting off the license to Munca Ovidiu also dropped our presence in the Black Sea region. It was a disappointing decision, and it brought up new strategic concerns.

During our set-up process, I had an opportunity to come face to face with the enemy. I met the senior Coca-Cola adviser I had contacted months earlier when the Kentucky group got the boot from Coke. He was quite direct in his comments. The man told me he had just visited Romania with a delegation of Coke executives, and we stood no chance against them. They were going to invest $300 million just in the Romanian market over the next few years and crush us and any other competition.

The battle lines were drawn. When I contrasted Coke's budget with the pocket money we had available for our operation, my throat went dry. We were facing quite a frightening challenge ahead, but I did not blink. I had long ago passed the point of no return. We believed in this venture and were committed to its success.

*Arrange things so that you can return.* About one month after we signed the joint venture documents, our deal received the blessing of the Romanian Agency for Development. We were officially able to open Sitaco for business under new ownership. It had been a year of continuous efforts. Jeff and I spent some ninety-three nights at the Intercontinental Hotel in Bucharest, and our work was not in vain.

During this year, we did not yet have direct involvement with the Pepsi business in Romania, but we did help local plants make various improvements. As a result, the sales of Pepsi-Cola, offered in only the 250 ml glass bottles, rose 50 percent, from two to three million eight-ounce cases. We left the place better than when we arrived, and that made conditions favorable for our return.

In the last month of the year, I was able to stay closer to home, because we had reached our objective of making everything ready to start the operation. I had birthed a new business in Romania, and now I returned home to await the birth of my first child with ever-increasing anticipation and excitement.

We survived the turbulent storms at the start of our journey and were now enjoying a brief period of smooth waters. We grasped on to those wise and ancient Viking laws and applied them without the knowledge that our world ancestors had discovered their secrets long ago. We brought to the project every ounce of our talents and resources and arranged matters so that we would be welcomed when we returned. Our journey was still in the early stages. The New Year would hold many new adventures. We could expect victories and setbacks, but one thing was certain. Our course was set, and we would not turn back.

# CHAPTER 6: FILLING THE SAILS

*The pessimist complains about the wind; the optimist expects it to change; the realist adjusts the sails.*

**—William Arthur Ward**

We launched our business, and we were picking up speed. Everything was moving so quickly, we had no time for fear. We glided across new waters as our sails filled to their full capacity. It was exhilarating and frustrating and heartwarming and ridiculous; at times the current was so fast we could hardly catch our breath. This venture was no longer an event. We found ourselves somewhere in the middle of a full-blown journey.

On January 6, 1992, we officially opened our business in Romania under the joint venture Sitaco. The very next day my first child, Yigal, was born. When I addressed our employees for the first time later that month, I told them I felt as if I had two children born at the same time. The first child was our operation in Romania. I had labored over it for a full year and finally saw it come into being. The second, my son, entered the world after nine months and a different type of labor that included an equal amount of joy and worry. The connection between Yigal and this new venture in Romania made it seem like more than just another investment. It was an entity very close to my heart.

Eli, our new chief, brought with him two managers from Israel to head the team: Jacob Katz, as operations manager; and Doron Engel, as marketing manager. The expatriate team was rounded out by Les Weiss, a chief financial officer whom we hired in New York.

The new team hit the ground running. They immediately looked for ways in which they could improve the existing operation. There were so many opportunities for improvement that it was not easy to decide where to start. Their first area of focus was the plant itself. The layout was very problematic, and the biggest issue was the fact that the company did not handle distribution. That meant vehicles of various sizes came to the plant to pick up the products. They waited in line for up to forty-eight hours, because production could not adequately meet demand.

Getting vehicles in and out of the plant was also a nightmare. The team observed the existing traffic pattern and noticed there was a funny little structure sitting right in the middle of it that served no obvious purpose. One of their first decisions was to remove that structure. As soon as the employees caught wind of it, they practically stampeded to the management office. They weren't against the demolition. They wanted to help. Employees volunteered to stay and work on the removal after hours if they could keep the bricks and other material from the old structure for their own use. Management granted their wish, and soon the structure was gone. The resulting traffic flow was quite a bit easier for drivers to navigate.

The next move was to find a way to create additional capacity to meet the demand as quickly as possible. Our plant contained only one bottling line, and that was not sufficient. The fastest and simplest solution would be to make use of existing bottling lines in other plants. If we chose that route, we would have to enter into an individual agreement with each plant to have them produce for us. A contract-packing arrangement, as it is called in the industry, was a perfect solution to our problem. Not only did it allow us to increase capacity, but it also spread out our presence geographically without costing us a huge investment sum. We didn't have the endless financial resources of Coke, so we needed to use a smarter strategy.

Our first contract-packing arrangement was signed with our old friends at Comaico. When our joint venture agreement with them stalled and we turned to Flora, they were left with an idle bottling line, so they were hungry to regain at least a portion of our business. This time it didn't take long to form an agreement with them. We settled on the main points quickly and agreed on a per-bottle fee for production.

We entered into a similar arrangement with Consuc, a beverage company based in Suceava, in the northeastern part of Romania. We were familiar with Consuc, because we had visited them several months earlier. PCI helped source a secondhand production line at Consuc with the forethought that the line could be used for Pepsi production in the future. Now that the installation was complete, we were ready to bring them into the fold.

We greatly increased our production capacity through our agreements with Comaico and Consuc, but we needed to aim higher if we wanted to lead the market. Later in the year, we entered into similar agreements with additional companies: Valahia in the center of the country and Arconserv in Arad in the western region. Arconserv was another plant PCI had helped to source a secondhand production line, so we knew the quality of their equipment was up to par.

By the end of the first year of operation, we had four plants plus our own producing Pepsi for us, and production lines were spread throughout Romania. Our investment in the other production plants was minimal to bring their lines to PCI's production standards.

We made quick and smart decisions that gave us a solid edge. It was a very positive start.

We had purchased a new bottling production line for Flora before we started the operation, and it arrived early in the year. Our target date for the completion of the installation was the end of April, which Pepsi's technical experts told us was an impossible goal by industry standards. We plunged forward, nevertheless, and came to another screeching halt when the installation team from Germany walked off the job. They claimed they could not work with our local employees. So much for a turnkey agreement! We picked up the pieces and trudged forward with our local workers, who had very limited experience. It was not an easy project for any of us, but we did what we could with our own resources, and we refused to accept failure as an option.

Eli and I talked almost daily, even though I was some seven time zones away in New York City. His first months at the helm included a number of tough decisions, and I appreciated his seeking my opinion before making his next bold move.

One day, Eli called me with a tough dilemma. He felt that he could not continue to support the canning line at Flora. The antiquated and unsanitary method of women shoving vegetables into glass containers didn't work on many levels. He predicted the problem might escalate, though, if he fired the dozen workers in the canning portion of the plant. It might ignite a strike among the remaining employees.

My suggestion was to close the canning line as planned and reroute the workers to other areas of the plant instead of letting them go. Eli liked the idea and went with it immediately. The entire procedure moved forward without a hitch. In fact, some of the former canning women eventually assumed responsibilities in our new area of distribution as helpers on the distribution trucks. They loved the change, because it gave them an opportunity to get out of the gloom of the production line and into the fresh air.

Another gigantic hurdle for our new venture was information systems. There was not a single computer in the company. The entire accounting and reporting systems were done manually. We hardly knew where to begin when faced with this harsh reality.

Eli called me with a proposition, but he was concerned that it might be a conflict of interest. Since we were starting literally from the ground up in developing our information systems, Eli's wife, Zohara, offered to provide us with a basic accounting system for a very reasonable investment of $10,000. I immediately saw beyond his concern and gave him the green light to proceed. It was by far the quickest way for us to get started, and I trusted that Zohara would provide us with an excellent base for our information systems.

I shared that decision with the board of directors at the next meeting, so the apparent conflict of interest was out in the open. Nobody took issue with it. It was quite simply the best option available. The package laid a solid foundation for our company's information systems, and it launched a successful business endeavor for Zohara, based on the work she did for us.

By mid-April, our new production line was ready to go. Pepsi's technical experts were astonished. According to them, we broke the all-time record for such a project by completing it in less than two and a half months. Our naiveté paid off. We were completely unaware of the impossibility of the task! We had nothing established as a benchmark, because it was the first project of its kind for almost everyone involved. It was a remarkable achievement, and our own local employees attained it. We turned our faces into the strong wind and watched the sails fill above us.

We were brimming with excitement over our successes in the first few months. Now, it was time to show off a little. On May 2, we welcomed a delegation of PCI executives to Romania. They came directly from the inauguration of the Pepsi operation in Israel, and we wanted to give them the royal treatment. That proved to be a mistake.

The delegation included David Jones, the division president; Dieter Neumann, the area vice president responsible for most of Eastern Europe; Hans Promberger, who reported to Dieter; and Josef, who was by that time one of our biggest fans.

Eastern Europe had been recently placed in a newly formed division of PCI. Headquartered in Vienna, it included some seventy countries in Europe, the Middle East, Africa, and other areas. It was a gigantic division. We were a very small fish in a very big pond.

We wanted to impress the delegation, so when they arrived we took them straight to Elizabeta Palace, which was once owned by the royal family and could now be rented out for high-level executives. Unfortunately, our plan backfired. It was the first impression of Romania for many of these executives, and they ended up thinking the place was in much better shape that it really was. Dieter had not even glimpsed the market, but he immediately suggested we should build as much capacity as we could to meet the huge demand he assumed we would undoubtedly encounter. We spent the rest of the trip attempting in vain to explain the realities of commerce in Romania to the PCI delegation.

In spite of our initial misstep, the second day of their visit was a momentous occasion. We held a ceremony at the plant to mark the opening of our new production line. The Romanian TV channel eagerly covered this historical event of the first PET production line in Romania. It was quite newsworthy in the country and in the beverage industry as a whole. Not only did it mark the introduction of the first nonreturnable package in Romania, it also introduced the first multi-serve package in the form of a 1.5 liter bottle. With this event, we initiated a tradition of "firsts" that would continue for many years to come.

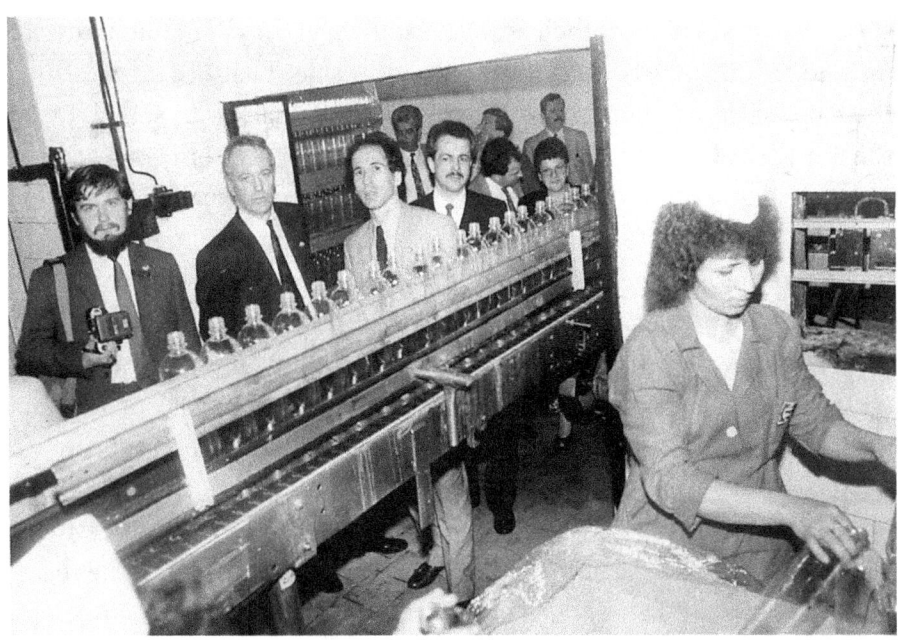

Misu Negritoiou was one of our distinguished guests at the ceremony. He had returned from his assignment as commercial attaché in New York and was becoming a rising star in local politics.

We had conquered the issue of capacity for the time being and celebrated our victory in grand style. Now, it was time to address distribution. Again, we started from the ground up. The plants previously had nothing to do with distribution, so we had no trucks or systems in place.

Eli attacked the problem strategically by visiting our neighboring Pepsi operation in Turkey. He met with the legendary Meli Sipahioolu, or Mr. Meli, as he is referred to by everyone, whose bottling operation had won the prestigious PCI Bottler of the Year award three times—an award presented annually to the bottler that Pepsi deems to be the best worldwide. Eli thought it wise to learn about distribution from the leader of the pack.

Eli visited Meli in Istanbul, and after a tough negotiation process, he came away with five secondhand delivery trucks. It was a mediocre start, but a start nonetheless. We used the trucks in Bucharest to initiate an unsophisticated method of van sale. That meant we filled the vans with product and sent them into the market to sell right off the van. It was far from a polished distribution system, but at least we had reversed the direction of the flow of product. We were going into the market instead of having the market come to us.

Marketing had been a forbidden word in the old communist regime. It was an evil capitalist tool that could not be utilized. Now, Romania was headed for an open market economy, and we needed to create a positive impression of marketing in order to get our product into a highly visible spot. That was a tricky line to walk, considering we were one of the two giants battling the cola wars. There were the "reds" (Coke) and the "blues" (Pepsi), and if you belonged to one of those clans, you made a total and uncompromising commitment to the team. We had to be ruthless in our competition but appealing in the market.

The cola wars were fought on multiple battlefields, and the front line was marketing. The Coca-Cola Company and PepsiCo spent huge sums of money to develop strategic advertising campaigns for worldwide use in order to give their brands a consistent image. As a bottler, we were obliged to use only the marketing materials developed by the brand owner or specifically approved local materials.

A "look book" was put out every year by PCI, and it spelled out the strict rules of using the Pepsi brand. Unfortunately, PepsiCo had a habit of tweaking its logo slightly to adapt to the dynamic world of consumer goods. A few months into our operation, Pepsi altered its logo again. It may have been a minor adjustment for Pepsi marketing executives, but it struck quite a blow to our young company. We had to change the logo everywhere it appeared.

It was impossible for us to modify the embossed logo on our existing large inventory of glass bottles. Did that mean the bottles were unusable? Then, there was the beautiful gift of our illuminated Pepsi sign that hung proudly in University Square. Pepsi had produced it for us just a few months previously. In an instant, it became a relic of the past.

The next blow in the cola wars came swiftly. We got a sobering look at our enemy, and it was clear we were in for one heck of a battle. Our strategy was to use our limited resources to create a unified team that would manage the market in Romania. Coca-Cola took a divide-and-conquer approach. They divided the country into sections and initiated a three-pronged attack.

The Coca-Cola Company itself handled the center of Romania, including Bucharest. One of Coke's strongest bottlers, the Leventis group based in Greece, managed the western part of the country. A Turkish Coke bottler based in Izmir piloted the eastern part of the country, including the Black Sea coastal region. Each of the three management teams brought its own resources, expertise, and large sums of money for investment.

We searched frantically for every possible way to maximize our modest investment, purchasing mostly secondhand equipment and trucks, using old multicolored crates for distribution, and, even worse, reusing the faded glass bottles from the old system. I personally spotted manufacturing dates going back to 1970 on some of our bottles!

Our enemy brought with them shiny new weapons. They had state-of-the-art bottling equipment, shiny red Coca-Cola distribution trucks, and bright red plastic bottle cases. Even their glass bottles were all newly manufactured.

We thought we would have the advantage, because the Pepsi brand was known to the Romanian consumer under the old regime. That advantage quickly became a handicap. We were connected to a past they would rather forget. We were old and outdated. Coke was the future. It was new and spotless. We were clearly outgunned, but our resolve did not waiver.

The economic reality in Romania presented yet another challenge. From 1991 on, the Romanian economy was in a state of high inflation and rapid depreciation of the local currency against the U.S. dollar. In 1992, inflation was running at an annual rate of 200 percent, and the leu had depreciated 40 percent by midyear. It created a situation where prices needed to be updated constantly.

Luckily, given the high demand for our products, the market absorbed those changes. A more significant problem was getting a hold of hard currency. A large component of our cost structure was not yet available in Romania. Pepsi concentrate and other raw materials needed to be imported and paid for in dollars, which were very difficult to obtain.

There were two ways to exchange lei to dollars: participate in a government auction or generate goods to export. Government auctions were limited. The government was selling a little bit every day, but they capped the amount because of their limited hard currency reserves. It was not a viable option, because we required quite a bit more cash. We decided to concentrate on exports. They weren't impossible, but they were very difficult to generate.

PCI had a strong global trading division that was created for the purpose of helping bottlers around the world deal with this very problem, but they never managed to generate export activities for us. We exhausted our limited connections by getting involved in exporting sheep, household items, jam, and anything else we could get our hands on. We advanced money to the producer of the goods and then collected hard currency when the goods were delivered and paid for by the foreign partner.

To say that this activity increased our risk in the market would be quite an understatement. It was a constant gamble. There was one case where the sheep we paid for could not be delivered, and a good part of our advance payment vanished. The exciting and diverse aspects of doing business in Romania were sometimes more than we desired.

During the Fourth of July weekend, I was on vacation with my wife, my son, and my parents when we were notified that my beloved grandmother, Blanche, had passed away. We rushed to Israel for the week of mourning. I felt very grateful for her long life and that she saw the birth of Yigal and even had an opportunity to spend a little bit of time with him before she died.

After the mourning period, I needed to visit the operation in Romania, so my wife, Ravit, came along. It was her first visit to the country, some eighteen months after my inaugural trip, and I was eager to view Romania through her fresh eyes. Our trip allowed me to gain some perspective on all of the development the country had seen in a year and a half. I appreciated the opportunity to mentally review our progress while I showed Ravit around.

Unfortunately, my wife's first experience with Romania was laced with a few less-than-ideal circumstances. Ravit had some difficulty finding options that would adhere to her dietary restrictions; ironically, the choice of beverages was one of her concerns. She drank only non-carbonated water, and all the drinkable water available in Romania at the time was fizzy, as their mineral water is naturally carbonated.

Ravit also had an unpleasant experience with one of the locals. She was browsing in a shop in Bucharest when a gypsy woman stole her purse. It was not at all an uncommon occurrence, but it was certainly not an event I wanted her to experience on her first visit to Romania.

In the fall, Jeff, Eli, and I visited Mr. Meli's Pepsi bottling operation in Turkey with the objective of learning more from the experienced and successful Pepsi bottler. Meli was very friendly and instructed his staff to cooperate with our needs to the fullest. The most important lesson Meli taught us was that we don't have to be shiny and new in order to be competitive. We toured his main plant in Istanbul and the marketplace. His operation was not sparkling new and spotless like our competitors at Coca-Cola. He used the old multicolored crates, just like we did, and his glass bottles also displayed the outdated logo. Nevertheless, Meli's Pepsi operation was very successful in combating the competition in Turkey. He had strategies that transcended what money could buy, and we hoped to learn about them.

When the business part of our trip was complete, we had a half day to spare, so we asked a guide to show us around the old part of Istanbul. It was such an intriguing city. One of the perks of our jobs was the opportunity to visit unique locations and experience cultures around the world. Standing in the middle of the old Turkish Bazaar, I not only learned about the traditions of Turkey, I also gained some valuable insight on Eli.

After walking around for a few minutes, we realized Eli was not with us. I found him moments later standing next to a small kiosk and negotiating with a tiny elderly woman for a set of miniature screw-drivers. He haggled with the woman for what seemed like forever until he finally got her to reduce her "outrageous" asking price by one-third, from thirty-seven to twenty-five cents. That was my first personal encounter with Eli's extraordinary negotiating skills and his thrill at exercising them whenever an opportunity presented itself. I was glad he was on our side!

In October, we played a key role in the most exciting event the country had seen since the revolution: a Michael Jackson concert! It was part of a worldwide concert tour sponsored by Pepsi, and Michael Jackson was then at the height of his career. As the local bottler, we co-ordinated the visit and certain administrative aspects of the concert.

Demand for tickets was unbelievable. Requests came at us from all members of society, including high-level politicians. We played up the entire event and built a marketing campaign around it. The day before the concert, the star addressed a sprawling crowd from the balcony of what is now called the People's Palace. This monstrous structure is the second largest in the world, behind the Pentagon. Ceausescu built it as his last megalomania project before he was overthrown. In fact, the old dictator never got a chance to address his subjects from its balcony. Michael Jackson  was the first to do the honors.

The concert was a smashing success. HBO chose to broadcast this one performance in the United States, for which Michael Jackson received $20 million on top of the large fee he got from PepsiCo for the tour. The exposure for Pepsi was enormous—a great victory for our ever-growing operation.

The day after the concert, Eli and Josef took a few small orphaned children to meet Michael Jackson. They handed Mr. Jackson a company check for $10,000, which he then "donated" to a charity for orphans in Romania. We were advancing various aspects of our business, gaining more exposure, and giving back to our community. It looked like we found our own three-pronged attack.

In November, we stacked up another first by launching the first international non-cola brands. We introduced both 7-Up and Mirinda simultaneously, paving a new path in our development of the beverage industry in Romania. We now boasted a small portfolio of carbonated beverages, and our aim was to find ways to expand it.

Our first year of operation was rapidly ending. It felt as if we had run a very long race at breakneck speed. Panting and weary, we looked back over the year—we took a moment to journal our journey. PCI put together a monthly chart of our sales, and it was the most beautiful image we had seen since the birth of our organization.

The chart displayed the evolution of twelve months of trailing sales, and we saw a solid staircase of growth to prove our success. Our total volume for the first year grew over 100 percent from the previous year. With all the difficulties we encountered, we still managed to turn a profit.

I took advantage of the December holidays to visit family in Israel, but my trip was not a complete vacation. Eli called me a few weeks before I left to tell me he had received a visit from a representative of a juice manufacturing company based in Israel. They were considering introducing their brand in Romania and looking to partner with a strong beverage company that was already active in that market.

Eli asked me to schedule a meeting with them while I was in Israel. The company was Gat Canneries, and their brand name was Prigat, which means "the fruit of Gat" in Hebrew. I visited their plant and was very impressed by their state-of-the-art juice manufacturing operation. Gat Canneries was owned by two kibbutzim, which split off in the 1950s over a bitter ideological rift related to the old Soviet Union.

The history of the cannery played out like a soap opera, and the characters were equally colorful. I met Moshe Arbel, the representative who visited Eli in Romania. He was actually born in Romania and immigrated to Israel as an orphaned child after World War II. This possible new venture would be an opportunity for him to return to his homeland and create an active business there. I was also introduced to Shaul Horowitz, the company's CEO, and Yossi Bueno, an Israeli businessperson who had been active in Romania since before the revolution.

We discovered immediately that our companies were compatible. We had a number of common interests and could be of great help to one another. We agreed to commence talks on a joint operation in Romania after the first of the year. Our underdog company now had yet another exciting opportunity to pursue in our second year of operation.

# CHAPTER 7: BATTLE SCARS AND BANNER DAYS

*The truth of the matter is that you always know the right thing to do. The hard part is doing it.*

**—Norman Schwarzkopf**

We started 1993 at the same level of excitement we had when the previous year ended. In February, a delegation of senior executives at PCI visited us again, and this time the delegation included the division president, David Jones. During a festive dinner at the beautiful Writers' House, he shared with us that our operation won the nomination of the division for PepsiCo's Bottler of the Year Award.

We were stunned. In our first year of operation, we were the leaders. We won the top bottler nomination in PCI's largest division, comprising seventy-one countries. We would now be compared to the leaders of four other divisions that spanned the globe, and the worldwide award would be presented at a lavish ceremony. The nomination gave us instant exposure and recognition from top PCI and PepsiCo brass. We could not have possibly envisioned a better start to our business.

There was not much time to bask in the glow of success. We were still battling Coke on as many fronts as possible, and one tactic we set into motion early in the year was to expand our product portfolio.

In May, Valahia, one of our contract packers, produced the first one-liter, returnable glass bottle in the market. That expanded the multi-serve package variety and provided a less-expensive product than the 1.5 liter PET. We accompanied the launch of this new product with a locally produced advertising campaign that featured a Romanian TV personality. The campaign became very popular and marked the beginning of many creative and bold new Pepsi campaigns in the country.

The most intense battle over consumer attention was being fought at the point of sale. Consumers were not interested in a warm soft drink, so we were looking for ways to give them the ice-cold Pepsi they desired. It was not uncommon to see kiosks selling soft drinks out of buckets of ice, but we sensed it was time to introduce something a little less primitive.

The introduction of coolers was the answer, but it came with a hefty price tag. Each cooler, depending on size, cost anywhere from a few hundred U.S. dollars to over a thousand dollars. We purchased the coolers and then offered to sell them to our customers. They took the bait and bought them, which allowed us to strategically place branded Pepsi coolers at crucial sale locations.

Our luck didn't last long. Soon our customers caught on to the fact that the custom in the industry was that these coolers were given "on loan" at no additional expense to them. They realized it was far more important to us than it was to them to offer the beverage in a state-of-the-art branded cooler. The entire cost was left up to us, and when we calculated how many of these things we needed to place in the market, coolers quickly became the most significant component of our annual investment budget.

Once again, our competitor's vast resources came into play. The cumulative number of Coca-Cola coolers placed at points of sale far exceeded what we could afford. Soon we were outnumbered.

Economic conditions in Romania also continued to be difficult. Inflation was running at an even higher rate than the previous year, and the devaluation of the leu spiraled further downward. Nevertheless, our sales continued to climb. We were heartened by growth, but our optimism was shot down when we compared ourselves to the competition. Their much larger resources were starting to make a mark around the country, and the growth rate of Coke was even greater than ours.

In late June, we held our first board meeting in Romania. After a year and a half of operations, it was time for our board members to witness firsthand how our business was developing. We gave them a tour of the Bucharest plant and the marketplace and then invited them to a Fourth of July celebration at the residence of the American ambassador. As a company representing an American brand, we were honored guests.

The event was packed with international businesspeople, and we looked for new opportunities at every turn. Unfortunately, one chance meeting ended in embarrassment. We ran into our old friend Reese, the owner of our advertising agency and source of numerous successful and bold marketing ideas for Pepsi in Romania. Reese had been our ally and one of our biggest fans from the very beginning.

I happily introduced him to the board members, but he chose that moment to announce to Alan that he was dumping us. I found out later that Reese was lured away by the Coke organization for quite a bit more money. Our competitor strong-armed us by stealing one of our most brilliant warriors. The entire scene was an unpleasant lesson in the guerilla tactics that took place in this ultracompetitive industry.

On one of my trips to Romania later that summer, I was reading the *Herald Tribune* and came across a small advertisement that read as follows:

*The first western-style restaurant, Velvet, opened in Bucharest. Located behind the Bucharest Hotel. No phone number yet. Reservations by mail.*

Reservations by mail? Was that some sort of joke? Turns out, it wasn't. We rushed to test the new culinary sensation, eager to find new delights for our taste buds. We left nothing to chance and made reservations in person, rather than the suggested method in the article.

Our inaugural visit to the new restaurant named Velvet exceeded our expectations and raised the local dining experience to a lofty level. We were enamored and made immediate plans to frequent the new establishment. Then we were hit with another crushing blow. Velvet had signed an exclusive deal with Coke, and they were unable to serve our products. We were dining with the enemy.

This wounded us twice. First, because we lost the battle to sell our products in the first Western-style restaurant in Bucharest; second, because we were not able to enjoy their food as much as we would have liked. We intended to give our business only to restaurants that sold our product.

We pressed on through our disappointment and grumbling stomachs, and in August we added another facility to our contract-packing framework. The company, Westim Canning, was situated in the western part of the country. Christian Dunareanu, an ex-Romanian who now lived in Germany, owned the plant, which filled cans rather than bottles. Westim Canning put our carbonated brands into cans, thus expanding our product line once again. We now had a returnable glass bottle in both the 250 ml and the one-liter sizes, PET bottles, and the new addition, 330 ml cans.

At about the same time, we added a new PET bottling line at our Bucharest facility, which handled bottle sizes up to two liters. More importantly, we acquired and installed a blow-molding machine that took small plastic preformed tubes and blew them into full-size bottles. That was a significant development for us. Until that point, we had to import fully blown bottles from outside the country. It had been inefficient and terribly expensive—we were essentially paying to transport air. With this new piece of equipment, we reduced the production cost of our PET bottles substantially.

September brought another first to our operation. We introduced the first non-carbonated, juice-based soft drink to the market under the trademark Natural Champion. It was nine months after my initial meeting with the Gat people in Israel, and we were celebrating our collaboration with the first product to emerge in this new segment of the local soft drink industry.

Our expectations were high, but the introduction to market was rocky. Romanian consumers were used to having carbonated drinks. Their locally produced mineral water came out of the ground carbonated, they enjoyed carbonated soft drinks, and they even added soda water to their wine and called it "shpritz."

Here we were introducing a flat product with no carbonation. Consumers thought at first that the beverage had expired or gone bad, and they were skeptical of this new line. We had the complicated task of educating Romanians about the benefits of non-carbonated juice-based drinks. Finally, it started to catch on, and we developed a nice niche in which we were the sole player. For the moment, our looming enemy did not get involved in this segment of the market, and we were left to build our brand uninterrupted.

At the end of September, my wife and I attended the PepsiCo Bottler of the Year ceremony in Scottsdale, Arizona. It was one of the best birthday presents I have ever received, even if that was not the intention of the event.

A few weeks before the ceremony, someone from the PepsiCo Events Department (yes, there is an entire department dedicated to events) gave me a call. She had a few rather odd questions. She wanted to know the circumference of my head and my wife's waist measurement. I wondered why on earth she would require that information from us, but I've learned to trust PepsiCo.

We arrived at Phoenix Sky Harbor International Airport and were greeted by a Pepsi representative who showed us to a stretch limo that transported us in style to the breathtaking Phoenician Luxury Resort in Scottsdale. We checked into our room and found an assortment of gifts: a fancy cowboy hat for me with a beautiful accompanying Native American bolo tie, and a leather Western-style vest for my wife with a stunning Native American necklace to go with it.

Next to the gifts we found a note that read, "Please join PCI's president, Chris Sinclair, at his table for tonight's dinner."

Dinner that evening was an outdoor barbeque. When we arrived, we were immediately shown to Chris's table. He welcomed us warmly and then introduced us to the guest of honor. My mouth went dry as I shook the hand of General Norman Schwarzkopf. I would be sharing a meal with the man who had led the Gulf War against Iraq only a couple of years earlier. General Schwarzkopf was an immensely popular war hero, and I was flabbergasted to have the opportunity to spend an evening with him.

We next found out that PepsiCo had brought in two top country stars for the entertainment portion of the evening. The entire experience was out of this world.

The next morning, General Schwarzkopf treated us to one of the most inspiring speeches I have ever heard. He talked about leadership, which was the overarching theme of the event. I didn't move a muscle as I absorbed every word he uttered. I felt as though I was part of something quite extraordinary when I listened to this man impart his wisdom to the audience.

We were then pampered even further when PCI gave us all a choice of leisure activities in the afternoon. My wife and I opted for a gentle rafting experience. Dieter Neumann and his wife, our designated PCI hosts, accompanied us.

The celebration culminated that evening with the award ceremony. It was attended by all of PepsiCo's top executives in the United States and internationally, including the Chairman Wayne Callaway. Bottlers from around the globe congregated in a representation of Pepsi's divisions worldwide. Every division representative received special mention, and the entire audience heard about its achievements.

We did not win the worldwide award, but we received a nice trophy to evidence our nomination. Unfortunately, there was no inscription to suggest the origin of the award.

My wife and I returned to our room exhausted from the lavish celebration. It had been a banner day, even if we didn't grab the big brass ring...this time. We discovered another little surprise waiting for us when we opened the door: a box and a note. I was beginning to wonder if I had fallen down the rabbit hole and landed in Alice in Wonderland's realm with all of the packages and notes appearing. I unfolded this latest message:

*This box will help you carry the trophy back to your home country. In it you will find a screwdriver to help open and close it...*

A helpful little note, and since it was the only written evidence I had regarding our company being nominated for PepsiCo's top prize, I framed it. We put it on display at our Bucharest plant next to the trophy.

Another full year of victories and losses ended. We tallied many achievements in addition to our prestigious nomination: our sales volume doubled for a second year in a row, and our profit was more than 3.5 times that of the first year. We were beginning to benefit from economy of scale.

Our pride in these achievements was negated slightly when we learned that Coke grew at a much larger pace that year and had started to create a gap between us. The challenge for year three was before us. We knew our enemy, and they could not be underestimated.

# CHAPTER 8: A YEAR OF TRANSITION

---

*If you do not change direction, you may end up where you are heading.*

**—Lao Tzu**

---

We began 1994 much the same way the previous year ended, but it would turn out to be a year of significant change. Eli and his management team were in their last year of a three-year contract, and that meant we needed to start planning for a transition. I had grown very comfortable with Eli's leadership and his managerial capabilities. I was concerned about the hole that would be created when he departed and felt the situation called for my being closer to the operation.

I had been commuting from New York to Romania for three years. The trips were long but, on the other hand, they didn't happen frequently enough. The seven-hour time difference between New York and Romania was also a constant frustration in maintaining the lines

of communication. It was not easy to keep up with the operation from such a distance.

I finally came up with a solution. I knew the right course of action would be to move my family back to Israel and commute to Romania from there. Both countries were in the same time zone, and the flights were under two and a half hours. That would allow me to be in Romania as often as needed, and I would be readily available to supervise a new general manager.

I had already convinced my wife of the necessity of this move, even though the timing was not ideal for her. Next, I had to persuade Alan. I put together a detailed analysis that showed the benefits as well as the costs involved. It was a major task to get my proposal past Alan. We currently only had one office, in New York, and I had been an integral part of it for a number of years. I was asking to be based at a remote location that was not even the site of our operation. I also held other responsibilities with the firm on projects that were based in North America, and I would have to give them up if I moved. We carefully looked over the pros and cons, and Alan ultimately agreed that I should move. I started planning for our family's transition back to Israel.

Early in the year, we decided to reward the management team for winning the division bottler of the year award in our first year of operation. They did not get to participate in the ceremony that PepsiCo arranged in Scottsdale, so we felt it was important to have our own celebration. We planned to do something away from our home market, as tourism in Romania was still underdeveloped. Ultimately, we decided to take the team and their spouses on a long weekend in Luzerne, Switzerland.

The trip was a fun experience for everyone and a much-deserved commemoration of their hard work and dedication to a venture that constantly battled against the odds. I suspect the spouses may have appreciated it even more, having willingly left surroundings that were more comfortable in other countries and accepted a life in the rough and ever-developing environment of Romania for a few years.

After the celebrations were over, we jumped right back into work. The key challenge for this New Year was to find a successor for Eli. I remembered the arduous process of our previous hunt for a management team, and this time I started my search in Israel. Much sooner than I expected, I met a very senior executive in the local beverage industry. If I could convince him to be our new manager, it would be a great achievement. There were very few people with his wealth of experience.

I was thrilled to find out that he was interested in the venture, and we started the process of introducing him to our operation. He traveled to both Romania and New York and impressed everyone he met. The salary he requested was a significant hike from what we were paying at that point, but we decided he would be worth the investment. We agreed on terms, and I felt like we landed a big fish.

The switch to a new manager would occur sooner than originally planned, so my next task was to break the news to Eli. I wanted to do it in the smoothest way possible. He had been an incredible asset to our venture. Opportunity knocked when I read that Frank Sinatra would be giving a concert at Radio City Music Hall in New York. There was a special offer for a preshow dinner with a menu dedicated to his repertoire and great seats for the concert. Eli had been an avid Sinatra fan all his life; I could think of no better way to show my appreciation and have a private moment to talk to him about the transition.

I managed to get two tickets to the event and then called Eli and asked him to come to New York for a couple of days. I offered no reason for the visit, and Eli asked no questions. We had a most memorable evening of entertainment. Frank was approaching eighty, but he gave an amazing performance. The next day, I told Eli I had found his successor. Our conversation went very well, and he committed to making it a smooth transition.

Meanwhile, our operation continued to expand. We were introduced to a wine company in a place called Blaj. They had invested in a brand-new bottling line of high quality only to find out that, in order to be competitive, they had to sell their wine in bulk, not in bottles. When we came to visit, they had not yet produced one bottle, and the line sat idle.

A very happy general manager greeted us. It was early in the morning but, apparently, he had already been tasting the wine. He showed us their facility, which looked very well kept, especially the untouched bottling line. The factory even had an observation deck from which one could see the entire production layout.

At the end of the tour, we were treated to a wine tasting of the local selection. The manager was very proud of the wines and was justified in his pride. When we finished, they asked us to sign the guest book. I glanced at the last signed paged and noticed the date was some twenty years earlier. Evidently, one of the guests in the seventies was punished after making a comment that was not to the liking of the authorities. After that event, the book was put in storage and did not reemerge until after the revolution. We were the first new visitors.

Our tour was successful, and we later signed a co-packing agreement with the Blaj factory. We added their production line to our manufacturing fold, and our bottling capacity received another important boost.

Arconserv, the plant in the western part of the country that had been a co-packer for a couple of years, provided another opportunity for development. The management at the plant showed an interest in converting our arrangement to a joint ownership. We jumped on the opportunity; within a short period, we had our second joint venture. We named it Arsico, and our company owned the majority. There was one added benefit to the deal. We came to know their in-house lawyer, Valeriu Precup. Eli was so impressed with his skills that he offered him a position at our headquarters in Bucharest.

Valeriu accepted, and he became an integral part of our management team.

Our next goal was to have a manufacturing presence in the northern part of the country. The region, Transylvania, is where the Hungarian minority predominates. The largest city in the region is Cluj, and we identified a production company in a small town not far from there called Dej. I travelled to that region with Jacob Katz, our operations manager.

When we landed in Cluj, it was late in the evening, and I was quite surprised to see that an entire delegation, including cameramen and photographers, waited for us outside our plane. They somehow learned of our visit and our plans and wanted to interview me. I had to disappoint the crowd by saying that we were on a private visit and had nothing to share with the press. It was far too early to make any announcements.

We drove up to Dej and toured the plant. At the time, they were adjusting the layout of the plant to make it ready for a planned installation of a carbonated soft drinks line. We commenced discussions about a joint venture in which our side would contribute the bottling line, and the opportunity seemed perfect. They also had a production manager, Mihai Matyas, whom we quickly assessed as a very capable individual. The only problem was that we had essentially exhausted our initial investment funds. I was going to have to look for new sources of funds for this project.

I remembered well what Johann Rupert said to me back when the board approved our initial investment. His warning was that I was to never come back and ask for more money. Going back to the board was not an option. We needed to look for a more creative solution.

We considered the thought of raising money from third parties. An adviser on the holding company's board was a senior executive with a newly formed investment bank called Wasserstein Perella. He told us that they had just formed a local branch in Bucharest named Capital S.A. He introduced us to a young and energetic team at that branch, and our hopes were high that they might help provide us with new investors.

The Capital S.A. team was made up of expatriates and local executives, and they were eager to engage in a project of raising funds for our operation. The person in charge of the project was a bright young woman named Kathy Kress. We quickly developed an excellent rapport and put together a plan for a "private placement." In other words, we were seeking to raise funds from a select group of investors, rather than making a public offer that was open to any and all investors. The project launched into action, and our expectations for creating another first in our Romanian business were very high.

On the marketing front, we had two major initiatives in the works. The first was to sign the famous Romanian tennis player, Ilie Nastase, to be our local Pepsi spokesperson. Ilie's illustrious tennis career was behind him, but he was still enormously popular in Romania. Our vision of his face appearing on Pepsi posters around the country became a reality, and his endorsement was great for our brand.

The second marketing initiative was even more meaningful to us. We had a goal to become the official sponsor of the Romanian soccer team. Romania had qualified to the 1994 Soccer World Cup, an event that takes place every four years. Becoming a sponsor for the team would be a major coup. Coke had always been a key sponsor for the entire Soccer World Cup event, and therefore most of the countries who participated had the support of their local Coke bottler.

In addition, PepsiCo positioned itself as primarily an entertainment sponsor rather than a sponsor of sporting events. They had no particular interest in our proposition. It took a major effort to convince them that it would be a huge marketing advantage for us to support this national soccer team that was so incredibly popular in Romania. We finally convinced PepsiCo that it was worth the effort, and we became the only Pepsi bottler anywhere to sponsor a national soccer team.

This was not only a great victory for us, it was also a logical continuation of our relationship with the soccer team, as we sponsored the first match between the United States and Romanian soccer teams a few years earlier. We created a huge marketing campaign around our sponsorship of the team, and it ended up striking a blow to Coke in Romania. While Coke was one of the main sponsors of the overall event, their presence was almost completely negated in our market, because Romanians saw their team connected to Pepsi.

By midyear, our organization was moving into high gear with our increased marketing exposure and recent agreements that would provide expansion for Pepsi in several areas of Romania. There was excitement in my own home, as well. My wife and I were expecting the birth of our second child. Ayal was born right in the middle of the World Cup on June 21, and I watched one of the games in the delivery room while my wife slept during her labor period. Our healthy new son came into the world, and suddenly our household became a lot busier. We were blessed with two boys, we were frantically making plans to move, and we decided to throw one more adventure in the works before we made our transition to Israel. We went on tour with a band!

I was invited to join a wind concert band made up of musicians from across the United States on a tour of the Caribbean. I have been an amateur French horn player since childhood, and the invitation came from Dr. Lee Chrisman, my conductor during my college days at Boston University. It was a temptation I simply could not resist. I knew such an opportunity would probably not appear again, especially once we moved across the Atlantic.

The tour was planned for early July, which meant that our newborn boy would be just a few weeks old. The pediatrician gave us the green light to travel, so I joined the band, and our entire family set off on another unexpected journey. Three weeks after Ayal was born, our family went on tour. We experienced a once-in-a-lifetime trip that included beautiful music in exotic stops along a number of islands in the Caribbean.

Our adventure also had a remote connection to the business. We gave one of our concerts in St. John in the U.S. Virgin Islands. Our company was actually registered in the neighboring British Virgin Islands, and this was the closest anyone from our team got to the place at that point.

During those summer months, Coke kept the battle raging in Romania. They followed our lead and introduced their first non-cola, carbonated soft drink called Fanta, and they brought it to the market in their usual grand manner. Essentially, they painted an entire city orange. The city they chose was Craiova in the southwestern part of the country. Coke created a huge marketing campaign around this orange city that included building a pyramid right in the middle of the town—painted orange, of course. We had a new battlefield in our ongoing war with Coke.

Late one night in early July, I got a phone call from the incoming manager for our business. He and Eli had been implementing a transition plan for several months already, and they were just days away from transferring power officially.

"I'm sorry to tell you that I will not be taking this job after all," he announced. "I got an offer I could not refuse. I will be managing the Pepsi business…in Israel."

I was shocked. Not only were we constantly battling our fiercest competitor on our home turf, but now we had to face a company within our own Pepsi family that was causing us significant damage. I couriered an angry letter to the chairman of Pepsi in Israel, but it was clear that we needed to look for a new successor to Eli.

My first step was to share the news with Eli. I flew to Romania to speak to him. Eli is a man of great integrity, and he made it clear that he was not going to leave us exposed with no one at the helm. He immediately agreed to extend his stay by a few months to allow us time to look for someone else. It was comforting to face this issue with someone like Eli, who was responsible and dedicated to the venture. I immediately started my search for a manager once again.

While I was visiting Eli, Romania reached the quarterfinal stage of the World Cup. Ioan and I watched the match with Sweden on TV at his friend's house outside of Bucharest. It was a closely fought battle that went into overtime and ultimately had to be decided by a series of penalty kicks. Romania lost, but they were still heroes in the eyes of everyone in the country. Overall, they competed in their most successful World Cup appearance ever. It was wonderful to witness the throngs of Romanians streaming into University Square that night to celebrate their team in spite of its disappointing loss. Our Pepsi brand was closely associated with the triumphs of the soccer team.

I returned home to face another transition. On August 14, our family boarded a flight to Tel Aviv. This brought to an end a period of close to ten years of residing in the United States and opened a new chapter in my life, both personally and professionally. I had to give up all of the other responsibilities I had with Quadrant in North America to concentrate fully on the Romanian business. From that point through the next several years, I spent every second week in Romania. This was not easy for my family—my wife and especially our two very young children. I knew it was the right thing to do for the business. It allowed me to stay close and be more intimately involved with our business in Romania. Recent developments proved that the move was a prudent decision.

One aspect of the move that needed attention was administrative support for my activity. I was not going to have a full-time office in Israel or any hired assistants. Back in New York, I had a dedicated assistant, Jane Ryffel, who handled all of my needs. She was used to me being away on business trips and was a very independent and self-motivated person. Jane would continue providing the same type of assistance after the move, and that facilitated the transition.

The closest destination to Israel, other than the surrounding Arab countries, is the island of Cyprus. Though it is only a thirty-minute flight from Tel Aviv, for some reason, I had never been there. That would soon change. Eli and Jeff came up with an innovative idea to insert a Cypriot company into our holding structure. It turned out that Cyprus had a very favorable tax treaty with Romania that dated back to the old regime. It would afford us certain benefits if we put this new company in place.

Jeff and I paid a visit to the island to take care of the details of setting up this arrangement. One of the appointments we scheduled there was with an accounting firm. As we waited for the appointment, we watched a marketing film that was put together by the ministry of industry and highlighted the benefits of doing business in Cyprus.

Imagine our shock when we discovered that one of the stars of the film was our good friend David Jones, the PCI division president for our region. He spoke with conviction about the benefits of having a corporate presence in Cyprus and explained that PCI had decided to take advantage of those benefits and place their head office on the island. There was only one problem with the film: by the time we watched it, PCI had cancelled its corporate presence in Cyprus and moved its head office to Vienna, the same location where the regional vice president for Eastern Europe was situated, and the spot where we became a Pepsi bottler.

Our inside knowledge did not dissuade us from our decision. We politely continued to watch the presentation without comment. Then, we followed through and formed a subsidiary in Cyprus. In fact, we kept our presence there for quite a number of years.

PCI actually went through several changes that year. In addition to changing location, they also changed the team responsible for our region. Josef left the company the previous year, as did Hans, and Dieter received another assignment within PCI. Ken Newel, an Irishman, and Lori McKilwee, a Welshman, replaced them. These men brought with them a renewed enthusiasm and were eager to find new ways to help us develop our Pepsi business in Romania.

One proposition the new leaders suggested was to introduce a new type of packaging. It was a returnable plastic bottled called a PRB (plastic returnable bottle). The new packaging had been extremely successful for PCI in South America, and they felt it would be equally successful in Eastern Europe. The main advantage was price. With the PET bottles, the consumer paid the full price of the bottle with every purchase, as it was embedded in the price of one bottle. With the new PRB technology, the bottle could be used a number of times, so only a fraction of its cost was passed on to the customer—just like the returnable glass bottles.

We decided to engage in a survey to see how consumers would receive this package. In a country where purchasing power was still quite low, one would expect that such a proposition would be very appealing. We were therefore quite surprised when the survey results came in. When asked what their main consideration was in purchasing a soft drink, only 0.3 percent of the participants mentioned price! This caused quite a concern on our side, since the only advantage PRB was offering relative to the existing PET bottle was price. But PCI's executives argued we should ignore that part of the survey and concentrate on the fact that otherwise it suggested a very high acceptance rate of the product. I was not at all at ease with this argument and, as it would turn out, I had good reason to be concerned.

Ken and Lori worked very hard to convince us to introduce this new packaging. In October, we all visited the Pepsi operation in Hungary to review their PRB project. This was supposed to help convince us that it was a successful endeavor, but we found a PRB bottling line that was mostly idle. The reason was that bottles were not coming back from the market at the expected rate. As these bottles were sturdier than regular PET bottles, consumers were using them to store other liquids. That raised a significant concern about the size of bottle inventory we would need.

Later that month, Eli and I were invited to visit Pepsi's concentrate production plant in Cork, Ireland. This plant served over one hundred markets for PCI. The visit was quite interesting, but it was only an excuse to treat us to an event called The Guinness Jazz Festival held every October in Cork.

After a nice dinner, we embarked on a bar hopping tour. This meant that in every bar we stopped, each one of us had to finish a pint of Guinness before we could move to the next place. We were accompanied by Ken (an Irishman), Lori (a Welshman), Walter Schilling (a German), and a few other local Pepsi people—all, of course, well versed in the art of heavy drinking. Eli and I were not. That evening I consumed six pints of beer, although not all Guinness. It was a record for me, which ultimately led me to fall asleep on the tour.

The PRB project meant a significant investment in both production equipment and inventory of bottles and special crates. When we showed continued resistance, Ken and Lori told us PCI was willing to invest in the production equipment, leaving us with the obligation to invest in bottles and crates. What ultimately cemented our decision was evidence shown by them that Coke was about to invest in PRB capabilities. We had no choice but to go forward and try to be the first in the market to introduce PRB bottles.

Once we made that decision, I concentrated again on the search for a successor to Eli. Finally, the winds of success turned in my favor, and I was handed a surprising solution. I met Bill Doheny, a very experienced American executive who spent his entire business career in the beverage industry. He had changed sides from Coke to Pepsi as new business opportunities presented themselves. Bill had worked both in the United States and internationally and, at the time, he was working on an assignment for the Coke organization in Romania!

What more could we ask for? Bill seemed like a perfect match. He already knew the country and wanted to remain there. He was quite interested in the long-term senior position we offered. The negotiation process went smoothly, and we agreed on terms and a short timeframe that called for his taking over Eli's position in early 1995 after a well-planned transition period.

Adding Bill to our team carried an additional benefit. He planned to bring with him a couple of managers who had been working with him on the Coke assignment in Romania. They too would be up to speed on the industry in Romania and would require very little transitional training. I was tremendously relieved with this development and felt as though we finally found the perfect person to take our company to the next level.

With the victories, there always came a few defeats. The private placement project we were pursuing to generate more investment capital for our venture did not develop as we had hoped. It was one of the very first attempts to raise funds for a project in Romania, and that proved to be more difficult than we expected. The majority of the entities that we approached for this purpose were investment funds and the like, and they were not ready for such a risky adventure. Other investors had difficulty with the valuation. Many of those who were interested expected unusually high returns in exchange for the risk, and our company was not prepared to offer those terms.

Meanwhile, we had to make progress on our new bottling projects in Dej and other locations. I had no choice but to approach Alan. He reluctantly agreed to advance some money for the project as a short-term loan. The loan carried a relatively high interest rate and the expectation that it would be paid back out of the proceeds of funds we were still attempting to raise. We were on a slippery slope, and it would later become a large problem.

Our year of transition ended, and we marked another period of great performance in spite of the many changes. Our volume grew by over 50 percent and reached the milestone of over twenty million eight-ounce cases. That was tenfold the Pepsi volume we inherited just three years earlier. Our profits increased by an even larger factor and generated a healthy cash flow that helped us fund our growth.

Our growing portfolio of beverages was also shaping up to look like a serious beverage company.

On the competitive battlefront, Coke outgrew us in overall sales, but we won one very important victory. Based on Coke's own public statement, at the end of 1994, they were behind Pepsi in only two capital cities in all of Eastern Europe—Bucharest was one of them!

# CHAPTER 9: UNCERTAIN WATERS

---

*Without the element of uncertainty, the bringing off of even the greatest business triumph would be dull, routine, and eminently unsatisfying.*

**—J. Paul Getty**

---

After three consecutive years of very aggressive growth, 1995 presented a new challenge. How would we keep up this pace? We wanted to hold on to the entrepreneurial spirit that was an essential part of our success up to that point, but we were no longer a small company. We had to find an appropriate level of control that would handle the increasing complexity of the business. I was hopeful that our incoming management would be the answer. We spent a considerable amount of time and money to place that very seasoned team at the helm, and they would certainly rise to the challenge...or would they? Our future was uncertain.

I had a number of issues weighing heavily on my mind, so I called Alan and scheduled a meeting with him in mid-February. We decided that the main offices of Richemont would provide a good location for our meeting, now that we were residing in different countries. Richemont was the holding company that was Alan's partner in the fund, and their offices were located in Zug, Switzerland.

I gave a lot of thought to what I was about to discuss with Alan and prepared a detailed outline. I started with an analysis of where our business was at that point. We had reached critical mass, we had very good profitability, and we were maintaining a healthy competition with Coke.

Next, I covered the issues we faced. The management transition was an uncertainty, and the competitive environment was about to get more difficult. The giant Coke bottler, Amatil, had recently taken over control of central Romania from corporate Coke. That meant the battle could get ugly very fast, as they were a fiercer competitor. There was also the issue of our investment needs to keep up the competition with our rival Coke. At that point, we had failed in our efforts to find additional resources.

None of this information was new to Alan. Most of the analysis had been shared with the board at our previous meeting. My conclusion, however, provided a radical new view. I suggested that we consider selling the business.

We were at a high point in the business cycle, and the competitive environment was still clean. We continued to enjoy very healthy growth, and I believed we could get a nice valuation for the Pepsi business in Romania. The challenge would be to find a strategic buyer.

This was not an easy conclusion for me to reach, and I shared that with Alan. This business meant a lot more to me than just another investment. It had been a very personal project from the beginning. But I had a responsibility to our shareholders, and I felt this was the right decision.

Alan accepted both my analysis and my conclusion. We agreed at the end of the meeting to hire a financial advisor to find interested parties. At the recommendation of PCI, we got in touch with a group called Hass Financial that had a great deal of experience in assisting Pepsi bottlers to find buyers. The board approved hiring that group, and everyone felt we were in good hands.

At the end of February, Eli finished his three-year-term with the company and passed the baton to Bill. I asked Eli what he wanted as a parting gift, and I was a little stunned by his answer.

"Naturally, a watch," he responded.

Eli had been collecting wristwatches for years and had amassed quite a collection. I felt like it was a bit ridiculous to get him an item that he already had in abundance, but Jeff and the other people in our organization convinced me that if this was what he really wanted, that's what we should get him. We had a very nice farewell party, and I presented Eli with a particular brand of a watch, as requested. Then he was off to become the CEO of the third-largest beverage company in Israel. Our crew was changing, and a new chapter in our journey had begun.

Our competitor certainly did not take any time off to bask in their successes. They were busy on multiple fronts. First, they were getting ready to open two mega-plants—one in the western part of the country and one just north of Bucharest. Their goal was to consolidate their manufacturing into two giant plants, because the industry was moving away from returnable packaging into the one-way packaging of PET bottles, and there was no longer a need to have multiple plants around the country. They also continued to place large numbers of coolers into the market, and their cumulative presence was fast becoming a multiple of ours.

We had developed our juice brand uninterrupted for almost two years, but now that grace period was over. We learned Coke was about to introduce a new line of juice drinks called Cappy. Soon we would be fighting them head-to-head in that arena too. Finally, just as

PCI had warned us, Coke was about to launch PRB (plastic returnable bottle) packaging.

The Coca-Cola Company was so proud of their success story in Romania that E. Neville Isdell, a rising star at the Coke organization, devoted almost his entire speech to the "Romanian Story" when he spoke at a Beverage Digest conference that year.

Back in our camp, we had a few major issues to resolve when we made the decision to pursue the PRB project. The biggest question was what size bottle we should go with—the 2 liter that would be identical to our current PET bottles, or the 1.5 liter that would differentiate it from the PET bottles. This was a major decision. It would determine what production equipment we would need to purchase, the size of the molds for the bottles, and the inventory of bottles and crates. All of that added up to a sizeable investment, and we needed to get it right the first time.

We visited additional neighboring markets as a continuation of our research to learn as much as we could from their experiences. The same scenario repeated itself as we visited plant after plant where PRB lines sat idle or were working at a very low rate. My sense of foreboding increased as each visit confirmed the reality that there was a low return rate of bottles from the market. This meant that we would need a much larger quantity of PRB bottles to assure continued production, and this, of course, increased the size of the investment.

On the juice segment side, we had another big decision to make, regarding the name of our brand. We had been using the name Natural Champion since the launch of the brand a year and a half earlier, but when we tried to register the name, we hit a trademark issue. It was taken. A French company had already registered the name Champion in the food category, and even though they weren't actually using it, we couldn't use the same name.

We conducted a market survey and analysis and ultimately decided to use the original name of the brand that was used in Israel:

Prigat. In Hebrew it meant fruit of Gat, and Gat was the name of the company owned by the two kibbutzim. We felt like we were making a compromise in giving up the name Natural Champion that had been circulating for a year and a half but, in actuality, Prigat was a much easier name for Romanians to digest. It caught on quickly.

We continued to expand our manufacturing base by signing a joint venture agreement with a winery situated outside Constanta. That move finally gave us a foothold in the Black Sea area again, three years after PCI closed down its first production line there. The name of our JV partner was Murfatlar. On one of our very early visits to Romania, an American businesswoman of Romanian descent wanted us to sign a confidentiality agreement before she would introduce us to this very company. She thought it was one of the "best kept secrets" in the country. That quickly became an inside joke, because the company was no secret at all. Murfatlar was one of the premier wine makers in the country, and they had been exporting their wines for years through the trading arm of PepsiCo. Here we were years later finally working with them directly.

Our investment at Murfatlar was small, since they already had the right space for a bottling line, and our company donated a line that was moved out of the Bucharest plant to make room for a higher-speed line. A good move, that brought our total to eight manufacturing plants around the country. That was the highest number we would ever have, and it brought total production capacity to tenfold what it was when we started the operation.

Even though we struggled with a few big decisions, the year was progressing nicely. Our sales continued to show healthy growth, and we enjoyed a period of calm and smooth waters. So just to make things more interesting, our captain jumped ship after only two months at the helm.

I received a letter from Bill by messenger that said, "I'm afraid I am not the person you need to lead this company." He cited difficulties with the local management team and his inability to enforce his brand of management.

I was bitterly disappointed. We had very high hopes for Bill and his team, and we had invested time and resources into the transition process. On top of that, we were sitting right in the middle of an extremely busy business period. I didn't feel like we could start a new search at that time, and even if we did, it would take months to recruit the right candidate. Unlike our previous situation with Eli, keeping Bill on until we found a replacement was not an option. We needed a quick fix.

I consulted with Jeff and with Eli, who continued to hold a director position after his departure. The name that came up was that of a rising star Eli had hired a few months earlier as a regional manager for western Romania. Dudi Halfi quickly proved to be a very capable manager and was producing terrific results in just a short period. Normally we would not have promoted a relatively new manager into such a senior position, but we really didn't have much of a choice. We needed to promote someone from within the organization, and Dudi was the only viable candidate. We immediately got the board to approve the move and then approached Dudi. He hesitated a little bit but finally accepted the challenge. This ended up being another great lesson on our journey: expect the unexpected.

The June board meeting was fast approaching, and we planned a big surprise for the members. We now had a corporate presence in Cyprus, so we decided to have the meeting there and let everyone enjoy the place. It was quite a challenge to arrange airport pickups when people were coming from a number of different continents, but it ended up working seamlessly. Judith Kratochvil, our travel agent in Israel, handled the entire task. She was so dedicated to making it a success that she came along with a colleague to make sure everything ran smoothly. We stayed at a beautiful resort outside the town of Limasol, and our idyllic trip included a four-wheeling tour of the island. The event concluded with a wonderful sunset dinner.

The next morning, people scattered to their respective destinations, rejuvenated by our island getaway.

As soon as we returned, we were hit with another surprise. PCI announced that their CEO, Chris Sinclair, was going to visit our market in early July. It was a clear indication that we were attracting attention at the very top of the corporation. Of course, we were in the midst of planning the launch of a new product, so we decided to use this rare opportunity to upgrade the launch and get maximum exposure.

PCI carefully planned every detail of Chris Sinclair's visit; leaving nothing to chance. One of the demands of the visit was that Chris would meet with key figures in the country. We went for broke and requested a meeting with the president, Ion Iliescu. The request was granted and the high-profile meeting was scheduled.

Chris arrived on a private corporate jet and exited the plane with an entourage of top executives. The release that went out before our press conference set the tone:

*Pepsi International chief lands in Bucharest to spark the latest round in the cola wars...company launches new attack on Romanian soft drink market with a breakthrough product.*

The new product we were launching was Pepsi Max, which had been introduced internationally two years earlier. It was a breakthrough product, because it was the first time there was a sugarless soft drink that used a sweetener with no aftertaste. The patented sweetener was a unique blend of aspartame, a sweetener that was widely used in most diet drinks at that time, and acesulfame-K. Aspartame had an aftertaste but not when combined with acesulfame-K. The name Pepsi Max suggested to consumers that they would get maximum taste without the sugar.

Pepsi Max was an instant success in many of the international markets, and we hoped to continue its track record in Romania. We orchestrated a unique launch on the streets of Bucharest in addition to our highly publicized press conference. The center of Bucharest was blocked off, and dozens of street performers on skates promoted the message of the new product. The crowds that gathered received an opportunity to taste Pepsi Max while they watched the performers.

Next on the agenda was the presidential visit. I had spent four years avoiding politicians of all ranks, and now I had no choice but to accompany Chris to the president's palace. The meeting turned out to be very pleasant, and Chris assured President Illiescu that PCI was committed to the Romanian market. This contrasted with his pubic statement made at the press conference we had, in which he admitted that PCI had "left Quadrant alone and looked at Romania as a low priority."

Altogether, the first visit of PCI's president to our market was very successful. Immediately following the visit, I took a short flight from Bucharest to Sofia, Bulgaria, to join my hometown concert band on a weeklong tour of the country. It was not a business trip by any means, but I couldn't resist the urge to use that opportunity to see the Pepsi operation there and meet with one of our old comrades in PCI, Hans Promberger. After leaving PCI, he became the general manager of the Pepsi bottler in Bulgaria. When I called Hans to tell him about my visit, he only had one question:

"Where will you be staying?"

I told him the name of the hotel where the band had made reservations, and his response was slightly disheartening.

"This is like the Bucharest Hotel," Hans said gravely.

I required no further explanation. I knew exactly what to expect when we arrived: a large, dark, looming structure with an equally unwelcoming staff. When I checked in, the woman at the front desk seemed annoyed that I distracted her from reading her book. It was clear that visitors were a nuisance. The concept of service had not yet arrived. Hans was right; it was just like the early days in the Bucharest Hotel.

Hans and I had a nice dinner, and he took me to visit one of the Pepsi plants, which was located about two hours from Sofia. I didn't know then that I would return years later to the Pepsi operation in Bulgaria under different circumstances.

I went back to work refreshed from my creative outlet with the concert band and dove into a report provided by Hass Financial. They had been working diligently on our task of finding strategic partners and had finally found a very promising candidate who expressed a keen interest. It was a group headed by Fran Mullin, a top executive at the 7-Up organization in the United States. The group had made some money with the sale of their business and was looking for a new investment. They were clearly the type of buyer we sought. They had expertise in the beverage industry and appropriate financial resources.

PCI was aware of our efforts to find a strategic partner and would need to approve a handover. They were very pleased with this potential buyer, so everyone was on board at that point. Representatives of the group came to visit our operation in Romania, and Hass Financial discussed with them in detail a range of valuations for the business. It all looked quite promising.

During the summer months of 1995, an event occurred that marked the beginning of a new era in the Romanian retail business: the opening of Metro. Metro was a large cash-and-carry chain, and this was the first store of its kind in the country. The occasion was so momentous that Romanians considered shopping in the store a form of entertainment. Metro was an immediate success, and it soon became our number one customer. Modern trade had arrived in Romania!

In September, we held our quarterly meeting in Constanta. It was the first time our board was able to visit this part of the country, and we used the event to officially inaugurate the bottling line in Murfatlar. The meeting took place at the main building of the winery and concluded—as would only be appropriate—with a wine tasting of their best vintages. The mood of the board was quite positive. We were inching toward the end of another record-breaking year in spite of all of the uncertainties.

There was one element that added to the uncertainty: PCI once again made a change in the way they were going to handle our market. Ken and Lori left the regional office to take on other responsibilities within the PepsiCo business. This time it was decided that PCI would have a fully staffed local office. In addition to losing two good supporters of our operation, we faced a new reality of having to deal with PCI on a daily basis. This could be a blessing or a curse, depending on the person managing the local business and the approach he was going to take.

I decided it was time to bring my entire family for a visit to Romania. Up to this point, my wife was the only one who had an opportunity to visit the country. I planned the visit very carefully, because the tourism industry in Romania was still in its infancy. I wanted them all to have an enjoyable experience and witness some of the remarkable beauty of this country where I had spent so much time over the last four years.

In early November, my grandfather, my parents, my wife, and my oldest son (who was three years old at the time) arrived in Bucharest. They stayed at the Sofitel, which was the first true high-standard hotel in Bucharest. We then traveled to Sibiu, a quaint little town a couple of hours' drive northwest of Bucharest. German Saxons inhabited Sibiu in the twelfth century, and it held a rich and interesting history. We spent one night there. Next, we visited Sighisoara where Vlad the Impaler was born. The story of Dracula was based on the legend of this prince. We spent one night in the resort town of Poiana Brasov, and on the way back to Bucharest, we visited the Dracula castle. The famous prince never actually lived there, but it is a spectacular sight, now woven into the folklore of the Dracula story.

The trip was wonderful, but there was one hitch. Winter came early that year, and the country was covered in a thick blanket of snow and frigid temperatures. Everyone, with the exception of my young son, took it in stride and enjoyed the experience. The highlight, of course, was the tour of our Pepsi plant in Bucharest. At that point, the plant was starting to look like a modern operation, and I was very proud to share it with my family.

Another eventful year ended. We had invested heavily in various areas of the business, particularly in manufacturing. The business was generating a very healthy cash flow, but we needed additional resources to fund part of the investment. In addition to new bank loans, we increased the shareholders' loan that the holding company gave us at the end of the previous year. The only reason Alan agreed to increase the loan was that we expected it to be short-term. The plan was to repay them out of the proceeds from the planned sale of the business. We all had a unified interest in maximizing the growth of the business in the face of our potential sale, so we came to this understanding together. However, there was a substantial downside in the event that the loan remained outstanding beyond the short term. That uncertainty would give me many sleepless nights.

The company performance in 1995 was outstanding. We broke every record to date regarding volume, turnover, and profitability. Given the two major management shifts that took place during the year and the increasingly competitive environment, we were thrilled with our success. Our journey withstood the uncertainty we faced earlier in the year.

# CHAPTER 10: CRISIS LOOMS ON THE HORIZON

---

*I am not afraid of storms, for I am learning how to sail my ship.*

**—Louisa May Alcott**

---

We experienced four years of significant growth in sales for Pepsi in Romania and we had become accustomed to this phenomenon. Then suddenly the wind was taken out of our sails. We never even saw a crisis looming on the horizon.

At the beginning of 1996, we fully expected to experience more of the same success we had seen in our first four years of existence. January sales came back below the previous year. That was quite a surprise. We broke our streak of forty-eight consecutive months of growing sales levels. It was disappointing, but the explanation I received was that the weather had been quite severe that month, and it had a negative effect on sales. It seemed like a plausible justification. Then the phenomenon repeated itself in February...and again in March. Romanians have an idiom: "In March, the winter has no power." They use it even if the weather is still stormy in March, to suggest that it is not something that can last. A severe winter could no longer be the scapegoat. Something was very wrong.

The competitive landscape in the carbonated soft drinks segment at that time showed Coke as the clear market leader with close to 70 percent market share. Pepsi was a strong second with 22 percent. All other brands combined, locally produced and labeled as "B brands," had less than 10 percent market share. A company called European Drinks had the largest share of the B brands at around 5 percent. In looking at this data, it was only natural for us to focus on Coke as our only legitimate competitor. That was a mistake.

Meanwhile, our PRB bottle, which we introduced late in 1995, was not producing the results we hoped for. Coke chose not to introduce the PRB packaging after all. We were alone in the market providing what was supposed to be an appealing proposition for the consumer. It wasn't.

We tried frantically to understand what wasn't working. Comments from consumers began to shed some light. They felt that if it was supposed to be an identical product to PET but at a cheaper price, then it must be some kind of lower grade of Pepsi. Their responses brought back the concern I had with the survey results prior to the introduction of that package. They showed that a very low percentage of Romanians cited price as their main consideration for purchasing a soft drink.

By the end of the first quarter, we were all puzzled by the overall negative results. PCI decided to engage an outside firm to analyze the market and find out what it would take to turn things around for Pepsi in Romania. They hired the Mars group, a consulting firm that had conducted many similar projects for Pepsi around the world.

Mars sent a well-staffed team to go around the country and look at the market firsthand. They produced an extensive report within a few weeks, and it confirmed something we already knew: we needed to focus much more on the distribution side of the business. Our manufacturing capacity had been built up over the first four years and covered our needs for the foreseeable future. Now, the name of the game was distribution. We did well in the major cities, but Coke had a far deeper reach into the rural areas of the country, and that was a significant part of the market.

It seemed like a simple solution, but spreading our distribution more comprehensively throughout Romania came with a high price tag. To initiate new accounts, we needed to provide some distribution assets—most importantly, coolers—and that required resources we simply did not have. The gap between the cumulative number of coolers Coke placed in the market and our figure had grown wider every year. By 1996, it was quite significant. We understood that the Mars study correctly assessed what was happening in the market. We just could not fix the problem with our limited resources.

At this point, we realized that our efforts to find a strategic buyer for the business failed. The group headed by Mullin somehow lost interest and disappeared. Hass Financial led us down the wrong path. We were so completely convinced that they had the right buyer that we did not even consider looking for an alternative. It was a very valuable lesson learned: never rely on one option, no matter how promising it looks. We should have done whatever it took to produce an alternate option.

One not-so-surprising result of our sudden decline in sales was added tension with PCI. The executives at PCI applauded our performance as long as we enjoyed solid growth each year. Even during our long period of aggressive growth, we were criticized at times for not doing enough. Our performance was always compared to Coke, and since our competitor significantly outspent us, resulting in a much larger sales base, PCI had the notion that our organization was a short-term player. They assumed we were only looking to make a good return on this investment and then leave.

When the sales results started to plummet, the criticism ramped up a level. The local PCI office that had been set up at the end of 1995 became a prime vehicle for pointing out our failings on a more frequent basis. They never offered much in the way of assistance, but they were on hand to provide criticism at regular intervals.

Our horizon was full of storm clouds, but the country of Romania was testing the waters in a bright new world of democracy. In May, they held local elections. These elections were viewed as a rehearsal to the general elections scheduled for later in the year. For the first time, there was a strong opposition party to the socialist party that had been in power since the revolution. Indeed, the opposition took control in many of the major cities in Romania.

In Bucharest, Ilie Nastase decided to run for mayor and chose to represent the socialist party. Even though he was an extreme-ly popular candidate, the general anti-government sentiment pre-vailed, and he lost. His participation in the elections, win or lose, was unfortunate for us, because we could no longer use him as a Pepsi spokesperson.

We continued to search for remedies for our declining sales. We discovered that Coke was also suffering a decline, although to a much smaller degree than we were. Both of us were losing share to local brands—mainly European Drinks—who were offering their prod-ucts at a huge discount to ours. The consumers were switching from A brands to B brands as a result of the tougher economic environ-ment that produced a decline in the average consumer's purchasing power.

We had to do something. We needed a brand that could compete in price with the local brands, and it could not carry the Pepsi label. We sourced cheaper concentrate and came up with the name "Fizz" for a new brand that we could position in direct competition with the local brands. The local brands were sold at something like a 30 to 40 percent discount to Pepsi's pricing. We chose to position Fizz at 15 to 20 percent below Pepsi pricing. We felt that the discount would give consumers an incentive to go with a less-expensive brand from a better-known company.

Fizz was put into the market, and we concentrated again on distribution as our primary area of focus. Our first tactic was to look at improving the efficiency of our distribution system. Jeff came across an ex-Pepsi executive named Peter Swanson who was promoting a software package called Margin Minder. This software had analysis capabilities that we felt could help us improve the way we were handling our distribution and tighten up the cost per case delivered. That was always an important point in our business because of its complex distribution system, but it took on an even more elevated status in our environment of declining sales.

The third quarter brought a new level of frustration. We were in the high season of summer and had not produced any better results. I felt that we had not been able to pinpoint the real issues we were facing, and I was not getting any answers from top management. At the end of one of my visits in early October, I sat with Jeff in a business lounge at the Bucharest airport awaiting my flight back to Israel. I shared with Jeff my frustration and told him that the only way we could get better answers would be to talk to lower levels in our organization from around the country. We needed to hear their thoughts on the situation.

Jeff liked the idea and offered to help organize an event that would bring our entire sales force together. We wanted to do it before the end of the year so that we could implement whatever we learned into the following year's plan. That meant we had a very small window of opportunity. This was no small effort. We had never done anything like it before, and we would certainly need some outside assistance to carry it out.

Organizational consulting firms were not yet a well-developed field in Romania, so Jeff suggested we approach Tmurot, an Israeli-based consulting firm with which my wife was affiliated. I was somewhat hesitant, but given the tight timeframe, I didn't have much choice. I gave Jeff the green light.

Jeff met with the founder and senior consultant of the firm, Yigal Or-Bach, and they developed an ambitious plan. It included a detailed outline for a two-day conference that would involve a few lectures and a number of discussions in smaller groups. It called for training some twenty moderators from our middle management ranks on how to facilitate discussion groups. The consultants who were to train these moderators were in Israel, so we had to set up a schedule for them to travel to Romania ahead of the conference and work with the chosen moderators, who were from branches all around the country.

Next, we had to tackle the logistics of finding a location, accommodations, meals, and so on for 250 participants—only one month before the date of the conference. It was a monumental task, but Jeff oversaw the entire process and remained in Bucharest for almost the whole month seeing to it that everything was moving along on schedule.

A few weeks before the conference, I suffered a personal loss. Shortly after I arrived in Bucharest for my regular visit, I learned that my grandfather had passed away. His health had deteriorated rapidly and unexpectedly over the previous weeks, and we were all unprepared for his passing. I took an immediate flight back home to attend the funeral. My grandfather was one of the people I felt closest to in my family. I loved and admired him very much. His departure saddened me greatly, but I felt fortunate that he was such an important part of my life for so many years and gratified that he was able to visit the operation in Romania the year before he died. He was so proud of what we had achieved, and I felt honored to bring him joy in the final months of his life.

At the end of October, I sent a letter to Bob Walker, the vice president for Eastern Europe/Central Asia, a market unit that PCI had recently created. I had been in charge of a Pepsi bottling operation for over five years, but I still had to introduce myself to Mr. Walker via the mail. This was a clear sign of the lack of connection we had with PCI's regional office ever since Ken and Lori's departure more than a year earlier. Of course, PCI now had a locally staffed office in Bucharest, but we received more criticism than support from them. Our relationship with the higher-ranking executives at PCI evaporated with the frequent changes in PCI's regional office, and I was attempting to reestablish it.

In the five years we were a bottler in Romania, the regional office moved from Vienna to Cyprus and back to Vienna (under a different structure), then to Budapest, and finally landed in London. That is where I sent the letter to Bob. In my letter, I gave a short synopsis of Quadrant's achievements as a bottler and also spoke about the difficulties we were experiencing. I made a point to mention that we could be dealing with the present situation a lot more productively if the relationship between our two organizations was one of true partnership. In the conclusion, I suggested a face-to-face meeting.

About a month earlier, I had received a letter from Craig Weatherup, PepsiCo's chairman and CEO. It described some of the difficulties the company was experiencing around the globe and spoke about a new approach they planned to take. The letter also introduced a new PCI president, Peter Thompson, who replaced Chris Sinclair after his sudden departure. I decided to use that opportunity to write back to Craig. We had never met, but I was on a mission to re-establish ties to the very top of PepsiCo. I was candid in describing our situation and once again suggested that only a true partnership between Quadrant and PCI could help us all through this crisis. I was hopeful that I could open a dialogue with both executives through this correspondence.

All too soon, the day of the conference arrived. We chose the resort town of Sinaia for the location, a two-hour drive north of Bucharest. It was once the seat of the Romanian king, and the old palace was still standing. Guests arrived to a beautiful setting, with the mid-November snow covering the ground and a dazzling banner greeting them for Quadrant's first "National Marketing and Sales Conference."

We invited a few special guests, including Eli, to the conference. The event started on Friday evening with dinner, and then the next morning the sessions commenced. All sessions took place at a beautiful structure called The Casino. It was reminiscent of older, more opulent times, and this was the first corporate function ever held in the place.

We made it clear throughout the conference that the company was going through a tough period, but the atmosphere remained festive. What we were doing was new and exciting, and the event united us. I was especially pleased to see the work of the moderators. They had never been engaged in anything like this before; some of them were quite junior in the organization, but they stood before groups of some twenty people, including members of top management, and mediated the discussions with the utmost professionalism.

We learned a lot during those two days. I'm not sure how many instant answers we found, but we created a feeling of togetherness that was not there before. We also inaugurated a tradition of uniting in this manner for years to come.

The last day of the conference was also Election Day in Romania. The right wing opposition, led by a university professor by the name of Emil Constantinescu, won. They ousted Ion Iliescu and the Socialist party, which had been in power since the revolution. When we returned to Bucharest, we watched the large crowds that gathered in University Square to celebrate the results. It was the first democratic transition of power in the country's history, and it was quite powerful to witness. We had heard over the years that Romania's lack of political stability was a liability for any new business venture, and here were throngs of people proving that notion wrong. Romania passed a very important test with flying colors.

A difficult year was ending. We lost almost one-third of our carbonated soft drink volume—quite a bitter pill to swallow after four years of continued success. The downturn in volume resulted in the first financial loss for the year in our history. We obviously had not yet found a solution to declining sales. The measures we took to correct the issue were all backfiring. Coke suffered a decline in sales as well, but their loss was much smaller.

The board of directors at Quadrant had been used to aggressive growth year over year, and they were now growing quite impatient with the situation. At the December meeting, we made a decision to make a management change. Peter Swanson, who had worked with us as a consultant to help analyze our sales and distribution system, would take over the job of CEO. Dudi would then be reassigned to manage our main plant in Bucharest. I was given the task of implementing the change.

In early January 1997, I received a response letter from Craig Weatherup. It was not a simple thank-you letter. He displayed familiarity with our operation and the difficulties we had experienced over the course of the previous year and stated that he discussed the matter with his top international executives. He offered no solutions, but he wished us a successful year and expressed confidence that we could find the "right means to move forward."

I made the trip to Bucharest to break the news about the new management change with a heavy heart. It was not easy on Dudi. He had been rising like a meteor in our organization, and less than two years after his appointment as CEO, he was asked to step down to a lesser role. Nevertheless, he accepted the board decision, and Peter moved into his new role as head of the company.

Our sluggish performance continued into the first part of 1997. It became more and more obvious that our problem was no longer Coke, but European Drinks. Its deeply discounted price took away market share from both Pepsi and Coke. The economy as a whole in Romania was experiencing a difficult period, and consumer purchasing power was on the decline. The timing of European Drinks had been perfect. They entered the arena with a much cheaper product that was supported by a good distribution system and a decent amount of marketing.

We had identified the problem much earlier, but the introduction of our own B brand, Fizz, did not yield good results. Technical problems with the product caused it to lose its color in the sun. Additionally, it was positioned pricewise right in between the A brands and the B brands. We thought at the time that was a smart decision—offering a third option for consumers—but the results did not agree. Fizz was caught in a no-man's-land, and consumers didn't buy into that proposition.

The other big disappointment in our sales performance was our PRB packaging. In reality, it was not even close to the great promise PCI sold us on. In this difficult economic time in Romania, the price proposition of PRB versus PET meant PRB had every reason to succeed, but it didn't. The culprit was a skeptical public. Coke had not introduced this package, because they chose to wait and see how we would fare with it. Therefore, the average consumer did not accept the new package as legitimate. If the market leader was not using it, they assumed there must be something wrong with it.

We were losing our status in the industry, and that became even clearer when I finally had a face-to-face meeting with Bob Walker a few months after I sent my letter to him. At first, I was gratified that he agreed to meet, but soon after our conversation started, I received a harsh reality check. He was a very experienced PCI executive and told us that at one point in his career he had been responsible for one-third of the world market for Pepsi. Our discussion was cordial, but it was clear right away that Romania was not a priority. We asked for some form of assistance from Pepsi, given the difficulties we had been experiencing, and Bob's answer was a simple no. He said there was not much he could do, because Romania was a "subscale" market for PCI. They were not interested in making any investment in our market.

Our dialogue with the local PCI office was never ideal, and our poor performance made the relationship worse. They continued shoving unhappy news in our faces by sending us periodic reports that highlighted the declining performance of each of the brands.

In May of 1997, I got a call from Alan. He informed me that, given the continued poor performance of the company, he had decided to get more involved. He was going to assume the role of chairman, and Peter would now be reporting directly to him. It was a severe personal blow. I had been the executive chairman of the company since its inception, and management had always reported to me. This business was something I started from scratch, and here Alan was telling me I was being pushed aside. Alan added that I would act as his vice chairman, but I was terribly hurt by the change. I had no choice but to accept his new arrangement.

During the summer months, a delegation from PCI, headed by CEO Peter Thompson, came to visit our operation. Because of our difficulties, PCI had decided to review its regional plans. They wanted to see our operation firsthand and evaluate its likelihood of success. PCI was even considering taking over our operation and buying us out. Peter had a discussion on that subject with Alan back in New York, and Alan was under the impression that they had agreed on a basis for handing over the operation to PCI.

The overall issue had a lot to do with the shareholders' loans we had taken out two years earlier. They were supposed to be for a very short period, and they carried a high interest rate and some penalties in the event they stayed for the long term. At that time, the loans were still outstanding and had mushroomed in size. Alan felt he needed to protect the loans, given the company's poor performance, and that put him and the rest of the shareholders, including myself, at odds. A sale at a low price would leave the shareholders with almost no value in their equity ownership.

In September, we had a board meeting in New York. Right before the meeting, Alan and I had a private discussion on the subject of the potential sale to PCI. It was the first time in our long business relationship that we voiced strong disagreement. Alan was prepared to sell at any price to cover his shareholders' loans. I thought it was a terrible deal for the rest of the shareholders, and argued that we should not pursue it.

Meanwhile, there was one unexpected positive development in the midst of all of this. An international investment fund called Regent had made very good returns in Asia, and they were looking to venture into Eastern Europe. They came across our company, did a relatively quick due diligence, and decided to become a minority shareholder. Our recent performance had not been good, but they believed we could get back on track toward success. It was an unexpected vote of confidence from an unlikely source. The cash was quite welcome too!

The business showed no sign of improvement throughout the rest of 1997. Peter focused heavily on sales and distribution, and ignored all other financial matters. The company was at the end of the road financially, and drastic measures had to be taken if we wanted to revive it. I talked with Alan right before the December board meeting at the Bucharest plant and suggested that we change our CEO.

"Who would take it over?" Alan asked.

I detected a faint breeze stirring the sails.

"I will," I answered.

# CHAPTER 11: SURVIVING STORMY SEAS

---

*We are all in the same boat in a stormy sea, and we owe each other a terrible loyalty.*

**—G. K. Chesterton**

---

M y suggestion to take over as CEO of the company was a decision I had to make. This business meant far too much to me to let it sink into murky waters. There was absolutely no one else who could, or would, take over managerial responsibility of this ship at such a low point in its cycle. I had never run the day-to-day affairs of a business before, but I felt I had to give it my best effort and guide the business through this crisis.

Alan agreed. Seven months after the phone call in which he asked me to step aside and proposed that he would oversee the management of the company, he realized that things had gotten substantially worse. Someone had to take managerial control. With Alan's support, the board approved my move to CEO, effective immediately.

I wanted desperately to have an orderly transition and asked Peter to stay on until the end of December, but that was not to be. Peter must have been hurt by the change, and he asked to leave right away. There was no handover of responsibilities. Instead, the helm was unceremoniously thrust into my hands without any adjustment period. I was immediately mired in the day-to-day business responsibilities. It was also quite an adjustment for my wife and sons when they found out I was about to spend the majority of my days in Romania for an indefinite period.

The actual job of CEO was more daunting than I could have ever anticipated. Performance in 1997 was even worse than the previous year. We lost substantial volume and market share, and the result was a considerable financial loss. Technically, the company was insolvent. We were unable to service bank loans that we had taken out during years in which we enjoyed healthy growth and profitability. We had no choice but to cut costs across the board. That also meant significantly cutting our workforce.

Eli had a full-time management position with a leading beverage company in Israel, but he came to our aid and committed to helping me. He was especially instrumental in handling layoffs. Eli analyzed every single position in the company and came up with a list of people we had to let go. In total, the layoffs accounted for almost one-half of our workforce!

It was an unavoidable task to make these cutbacks, but it was painful nonetheless. Many of the people we had to let go had been with the company for a number of years. It was a harsh decision to reward their loyalty in such a way. Eli spoke with many of the employees personally, explaining the grave situation in which the company found itself. There were other cases where we kept employees on but had to significantly reduce their salaries. It was going to be tough to build camaraderie among the surviving members of our crew.

One of my first tasks as CEO was to choose an assistant. A number of secretaries had worked for previous CEOs, but I felt I needed to start fresh. I promoted Carmen Popescu, who was working under one of our managers, to the position. Carmen, like many of our secretaries, had worked as an engineer in the years before the revolution. After the fall of communism in Romania, she made a strategic choice to take a lower-level position with a multinational company. She looked at it as an opportunity to earn more in the long run and have exposure to a more interesting work environment with multiple opportunities for advancement. Carmen was overqualified as an assistant, but she quickly became a very important support element for our business.

I was also very lucky to be flanked by two senior financial people: Moshe Blau, the CFO; and Leon Shachar, the controller. Both of these individuals had not been with the company long, but they were very aware of the grave situation we were in and worked diligently to find all possible opportunities to rectify our circumstances. Their support stretched beyond issues within their domains of responsibility to many other aspects of the business where they offered valuable solutions.

We rescheduled our bank loans and talked to suppliers about extending credit terms. We moved our headquarters to an unused area of the production plant to save costs. The vacated apartment soon became my home, since I was now spending quite a bit more time in Romania.

I sensed that I needed to stay very close to the marketplace to understand our situation more clearly, so I made a habit of spending one day a week with one of our salespeople on their daily sales calls. It allowed me to see firsthand our presence in the market, witness how customers perceived us, and take note of the way our competitors appeared in the market. Communication with the salespeople was not always easy. Many of them spoke very little English, and my Romanian was quite limited too. Nevertheless, the trips gave me invaluable insight into the business.

I could see very clearly that our distribution reach was weak, not just in relation to Coke, but also in comparison to European

Drinks. The latter was making their products available absolutely everywhere. In less than two years, they took their market share from 5 percent to over 50 percent. Coke became the number-two player in the CSD market, and Pepsi fell to third.

One of our sales managers related a story to me that clearly explained the situation. Her daughter would have (obviously) preferred to buy a Pepsi for lunch at school, but if she did so, then she had no money left for a snack. If she bought one of the cheaper European Drinks products, she would have change left over for something else to buy. That same exact logic drove many Romanian consumers to buy a B brand over Coke or Pepsi. It was hard to argue with that reasoning, especially in the tough economic environment the country was experiencing.

Given our low sales levels, another step we needed to take was to reduce the number of plants we were operating. It was relatively easy to reduce the level of business we did with our contract packers or stop using them altogether. In fact, we had already phased a few of them out by 1998. Our own plants were quite a bit more difficult to close down. One place I had to shut down was the joint venture with Murfatlar outside of the Black Sea city of Constanta. It was a difficult move, because we had just opened that plant two years earlier. However, the plant was simply too small and inefficient for us to operate at that point.

I decided that I must personally deliver the unpleasant news to the employees, so I drove to Constanta with a few members of my management team. I was warned that there might be some disturbances because of the news, but the meeting went eerily quiet when I explained our decision. The employees accepted it without any expression of anger or even displeasure. It reinforced an image I had developed of Romanians: when they suffer a blow, they bow their heads and quietly continue on. It was a striking display of survival, but that stoicism may also have been one of the reasons the old regime was able to remain in power in Romania for as long as it did.

In February, we attempted to rally the troops. We held the Second Annual National Marketing and Sales Conference for our company. It had been over a year since the inaugural conference, and I felt it was important to deliver an inspirational message in these turbulent times. I wanted to acknowledge that this was a very difficult phase in the company's life but also reassure our employees that we were going to survive it and emerge from the storm even stronger than before.

We put together the second conference relatively quickly, because we were able to build on our experience from the first one. We used Tmurot again, but this time we hired a local human resources firm to carry out some of the tasks. The most valuable benefit of using that local firm was getting to know Anca Podoleanu, who was the main consultant on the project. It was the beginning of a very beneficial relationship between Anca and our company.

When I gave my opening speech at the conference, I entered wearing a Pepsi sweatshirt and made my remarks in Romanian (with the help of a colleague who transliterated the text for me). Toward the end of my speech, I dramatically took off the sweatshirt, to reveal another shirt that said, "We are Quadrant." I wanted to convey the message that while Pepsi was a core element of our business, we were a beverage company that had to find a way to survive even if the Pepsi brands were suffering. The success of Quadrant was what ultimately mattered, and our goals were not always one and the same with Pepsi. In other words, if Pepsi was sinking in Romania, we would not be going down with the ship.

There was a second element that I wanted to convey in my speech, and that was a message of loyalty. Even during this difficult period, we were going to continue to invest in our business, and especially in our people. One area that sorely needed investment was the fleet of cars for our salespeople. The cars they drove were all old and battered. A small, locally produced car called Tico was new on the market, and we thought it would be very suitable for our salespeople. It was also relatively inexpensive. We bought a large number of Ticos to replace the old fleet, and I used this opportunity at the conference to tell our salespeople about our new purchase. I made the following commitment: anyone who stayed with the company for five years would own their car at the end of that period. It was a unique way to reward loyalty within the organization, and it allowed our employees to focus on the promising long-term goals rather than the short-term difficulties we were presently facing. We all left the conference with a new sense of unity, hope, and determination to survive.

Our next task after the conference was to bid farewell to a very valuable crewmember. Jeff, our general counsel, who had been closely associated with our company from the very beginning, made a decision to pursue new business interests. I planned a special send-off party and decided that the March board meeting would be the best time for the event. We rented a beautiful hall in the middle of Bucharest and even brought in a pantomime as entertainment to spice up the event. The mime did a special performance around the Pepsi theme. The evening was very festive in spite of the tough times our company was going through. It was a fitting farewell for someone who contributed so much to the early success of the business. Jeff, however, was not going to leave us altogether. He stayed on as a member of the board of directors.

Our strategy at this point was to search for ways to enhance our sales. One idea was to broaden our portfolio of beverages. We were even willing to look at products that we did not produce. Up to that point, we had only carbonated and non-carbonated soft drinks in our basket. We decided to analyze all segments of the beverage market and find out what opportunities we were missing.

We found several new prospects. The first was a beer brand called Gambrinus. A Spanish family owned it, and they were prepared to make us their distributor. Another was a dairy farm that produced milk with extended shelf life. A third was an energy drink called

Power Horse that claimed to be a strong competitor of Red Bull. We added those products to our portfolio.

All of these additions gave us only a distribution fee, so we did not have the full benefit of selling a product that we produced, but they helped us keep our heads above water. They provided additional income, and they made us more attractive as an overall supplier of beverages. This was extremely important during this period when our core brands were weaker than they had ever been in the market.

We introduced one additional beverage of our own at this time. It was a combination of juice and alcohol called Alcopop. This was an emerging segment in the beverage industry, and it became quite popular in a number of markets. Our excitement grew when we were able to register the name Alcopop as our own brand. We threw this product into the market with a giant splash by adopting a marketing campaign that was used successfully in Russia. We attached condoms to some five hundred thousand bottles. We felt that it would surely catch the attention of our consumers.

Most of these new products did not last long in our portfolio, but one other segment we felt was especially strategic for the long term. That one was mineral water. The market for mineral water was growing rapidly, and we needed to start carrying it in our assortment of products. A majority of the mineral water brands produced locally were carbonated, because that was mostly how water came out of the springs in Romania.

We found a brand of mineral water called Perla. A few entrepreneurs had developed it and financed it through a local bank called Bank Co-op. A senior manager of the bank was an old acquaintance of ours. He used to work for the Romanian Agency for Development, which was the governmental agency that approved our initial joint venture.

The bank found some "irregularities" with the initial investment and it was looking for someone else to take over ownership. After a short negotiation process, we assumed majority ownership of

Vitarom, the owner of the Perla brand. That brought us to the "three P's" of our major brands: Pepsi, Prigat, and Perla.

Another aspect of the business that we had to constantly reevaluate was our distribution system. Most of our distribution was direct, which meant that we were selling and delivering products by ourselves directly to the customers. In contrast, Coke's system relied heavily on local third-party distributors that accounted for a substantial part of their sales.

We decided that we had to expand the indirect part of our distribution. Our main task for accomplishing this was to find third-party distributors in less-populated areas of the country where our distribution was weak. I gave the task of finding the right candidates to Moshe Arbel, the Prigat employee who was helping us with special assignments. His fluency in Romanian, strong interpersonal skills, and most importantly, his entrepreneurial spirit, made him a perfect choice for this assignment. Moshe traveled all over the country and came up with close to fifty new distributors for us in a very short time. It was a meaningful enhancement to our distribution reach.

I accompanied Moshe on one of his trips to eastern Romania. We started in the northern city of Iasi, and I learned that Moshe's early years, right after World War II, were spent in that location. Moshe was born in a concentration camp during the war and then returned with his mother to her hometown of Iasi. His mother did not last very long after the war, and we visited the graveyard where she was buried. Moshe immigrated to Israel as an orphaned child after her death and ended up, years later, in Kibbutz Givat Haim, which was the owner of the Prigat brand. His involvement in our business ventures in Romania closed an important personal circle for Moshe.

We traveled south along the eastern part of the country to the Danube Delta. This area where the Danube River connects to the Black Sea after flowing through a large part of Europe is quite unique. It is one of the last large natural delta habitats in the world. We were there in May—a perfect time to witness birds coming back from their winter migration. The entire trip was fascinating, and I returned to Bucharest feeling as though I had received a second wind, a boost of hope for our future.

One evening shortly after my return, I was sitting in my office when in walked one of our young sales managers, Eusediu Margasoiu. I was acquainted with Eusediu mainly through our two national conferences. He was one of our star moderators. Eusediu had a request: he wanted to switch from sales to marketing.

I thought about his proposal for a moment. Eusediu had zero marketing experience. On the other hand, he was a proven success in sales. It seemed like a ridiculous idea, but I could see that change was "burning in his bones," so I went with my gut and granted his wish. One thing that our organization was able to afford its employees—even during difficult times—was an opportunity to pursue their dreams. I was not about to stand in his way.

Eventually, we started to see a bit of sunlight. Things were looking just a little bit better. Then we received another big boost: Eli ended a three-year tenure as head of the Israeli beverage corporation and was available to take on a new assignment. I jumped on the opportunity and tried to convince him to come back and lead the company. I knew he was the best person for the job, and his return would allow me to step out of the managerial job I had taken as a last resort.

Eli and I started to discuss the possibility of his homecoming. He was interested but not quite sure. Ours was not the only offer on the table either. He had a number of opportunities. We had a prolonged negotiation process. I told Eli that we were offering him more than a job. This time he would return as a partner in the business.

Late one June evening I boarded a flight to Bucharest after another long discussion with Eli. I was a little upset, because it looked as though he was going to opt for another business opportunity. When I arrived in Bucharest two and a half hours later, I received a call from Eli. He made his final decision: he was rejoining our company!

I was incredibly pleased to have Eli back on our crew. I knew it was the best solution for the company, but there was also a personal aspect. When I took over the managerial position, I had no idea how long it was going to last. It was a difficult time for my family and me. I was away from home for extended periods, and that took a toll on us all. Additionally, my wife was pregnant with our third child, and she was due in a month. Eli's return allowed me to be with my family again at this very important time.

Eli took over the reins at the end of June, and it was an easy transition. He was already familiar with our business, had been quite close to our operation during the six months I managed the day-to-day operations, and had three additional years of valuable experience with a beverage company.

I left Romania just in time to go with my family to New York where our third child would be delivered. Once the family was settled in New York and the doctors assured me that the baby would most likely not be born before the due date at the end of July, I traveled back to Europe. My first stop was Austria, where I participated in a short concert tour with my hometown band. Then, I visited the operation in Bucharest.

On July 20, I was sitting with Eli in the cafeteria at our plant when I got a call from my wife. Her water had broken, and she was on the way to the hospital. I boarded the first flight I could find, and sixteen hours later, via a connection in Zurich, I landed in New York. I missed the delivery of my third son by ninety minutes! When I arrived at the hospital, my wife was still in the delivery room with our newborn, Yiftach. It was a joyous moment, but I will never forgive myself for having missed the delivery.

At the end of that summer, PCI approached us with a new idea. They wanted to explore the notion of creating a regional bottler that would consist of several smaller bottling operations, including ours. In order to evaluate the idea, PCI hired the Mars group again. This time their mission was to cover a number of markets in the Balkans.

It was an expensive proposition, but we were already used to the grand ideas that PCI came up with from time to time.

We continued to have difficulty competing with European Drinks on price, and PCI was unable to offer a price alternative for us. Therefore, Eli came up with a new idea. He thought we should seek a cheaper product with a group he knew from his days as the head of the Israeli beverage company. Triarc was the name of the group, and they were the producer of Royal Crown (RC) Cola and other carbonated beverages.

Eli had tremendous success with the group when he was in Israel— turning that market into an extremely successful endeavor for RC. When Eli approached Triarc about doing something in Romania, they were quite interested in a repeat performance. We started a process of selecting the right brand for Romania. We couldn't introduce a cola drink, because that would be far too difficult a pill for PCI to swallow. Instead, we decided to initiate a series of flavors that would compete directly with European Drinks. Ultimately, we chose Kick, a secondary brand of RC.

As 1998 was ending, our team reflected on it as a year of new beginnings. It was also a year in which management responsibility had been split in half, residing with me in the first part of the year and Eli in the second. Pepsi brands were still down, but our overall turnover grew, and we even managed to secure a small profit. We continued to struggle, but we were starting to feel like we were headed in a new and promising direction. The company was going to withstand the challenges it faced, and we vowed that it would see better times.

In our planning sessions for 1999, Eli concluded that our organization needed to get smaller before it could resume a healthy growth period. He put together a budget designed to reduce the level of sales compared to 1998. It was a gutsy move and not an easy plan to sell to the board of directors. Nevertheless, the board approved Eli's budget. They put their trust in his vision.

We launched into 1999 with a series of changes. We decided to acknowledge that the PRB package had been a failure and terminate it. Instead of the PRB production line that PCI had given to us, we purchased an improved PET line that we found in France. We made this decision with the consent of PCI; the proceeds from the PRB line, although not very significant, went toward the purchase of the PET line.

We introduced Kick in the first quarter in a new attempt to fight the B brands. The Triarc organization gave us some great marketing ammunition in the form of several aggressive commercials that caught the attention of consumers. This time we positioned the brand at a proper price point. Kick showed great initial results and quickly became a meaningful component of our portfolio. Our Pepsi brands were still on the decline, so this was a much-needed boost to our carbonated soft drinks volume.

In April, we witnessed another interesting development at PCI. They moved the regional office responsible for our market once again. This time…to Milan. We had gotten used to these fluctuations and did not have any particular expectations about the latest move. Eli and I dutifully travelled to Milan to visit the new team.

We were pleasantly surprised when we met Massimo Ambrossini, the head of the new Milan office. We saw right away that he had a fresh approach. He expressed an interest in supporting our operation and working with us to see how we could get our operation back into a growth mode. It was a refreshing change from the last couple of years, and we were ready to renew a partnership mode with PCI. Eli and I left the meeting encouraged and sensing that this new development might signal a turning point.

By midyear, Alan raised the notion once again of selling the business. He felt that the company was stabilized and out of critical condition, and he thought it might be "sellable" again. Eli and I thought it was too early in the recovery period, and an attempted sale would cut short our efforts to rebuild value in the business. In order to bridge the gap between us, Alan agreed to two things: a minimum price level that would allow all shareholders to realize some value, and an incentive plan if we consummated the sale within a certain timeframe. I did not think it was the right time for a sale, but I was pleased that we were able to work out our differences and avoid the tension we endured on this subject two years earlier.

In August, I timed one of my regular visits to Bucharest to coincide with a special event: a total eclipse of the sun. According to international astronomers, the best place to watch this eclipse was Romania. The phenomenon stirred up quite a bit of worldwide attention, and a few companies even gave out special glasses to enhance the viewing of the eclipse as part of their marketing campaigns.

It was indeed an inspiring event. At around two o'clock in the afternoon, the moon completely blocked the sun. For two full minutes, darkness fell on earth at midday. I could see why in ancient times people thought this phenomenon signaled the end of the world. It was a surreal experience.

To make the event even more special, the world-renowned tenor, Luciano Pavarotti, gave an open-air concert in Bucharest to commemorate the day. Our company was one of the sponsors, and I went along with a few of our managers. It was a fabulous concert, and the overflowing crowd gave the famous entertainer a very warm welcome.

In the fall, Eli and I went to Milan again to visit PCI's regional office. We were surprised when Massimo gave us the news that his right-hand man, the person who had been handling our market since we met some six months earlier, was leaving. Massimo introduced us to his replacement, Antonio Calvano.

Eli and I immediately took a liking to Antonio. He was a lovable guy from the southern part of Italy. Even though he had spent much of his adult life in the middle and northern part of the country, he had maintained his Mediterranean character. We found Antonio's direct and candid style quite refreshing and felt like we were on common ground. It was the beginning of a wonderful friendship.

In mid-November, we signed an advisory agreement with a small, regional investment group to assist us in another attempt to sell the company. We established guidelines and gave the firm a mandate to look for potential buyers. One more such attempt was underway.

When Eli and I looked over the company performance for 1999, we could have viewed it as disappointing: sales were at their lowest level since our second year of operation. But that was a planned move, and the company actually turned a positive cash flow even at that low level of sales. We felt that we were positioned for healthy and sustainable growth. We had weathered the storm, and we emerged stronger and more determined than ever to thrive.

# CHAPTER 12: CATCHING OUR SECOND WIND

---

*Most people never run far enough on their first wind to find out they've got a second.*

**—William James**

---

I looked down at the title of the document that spelled out our plan for 2000 and realized we might have a slight problem.

*Bug. 2000*

The word in Romanian for budget is *buget*. I explained to the management team that their choice of words was unfortunate considering the computer hazard that had the entire world in a panic as we faced the new millennium. Nevertheless, just as the change from 1999 to 2000 resulted in no catastrophic world technology issues, the heading on our new budget had no negative effect on our performance.

We started the year with an aggressive campaign: for every two-liter bottle of Pepsi our consumers bought, they received a free bottle of our mineral water brand, Perla. We felt consumers would view this as a significant savings. They would see the retail price of Perla as their gain, whereas for us the actual cost would be much smaller. The campaign scored an immediate success. Sales of the Pepsi brand soared, and we increased consumer exposure to our water brand.

In mid-March, we held another national marketing and sales conference. This time we changed the location to Poiana Brasov, a famous ski resort three hours north of Bucharest. The theme for the conference was *Team Building*—very appropriate for our company at this stage of the game. Anca was now our in-house human resources director and ran the entire program for the event. Our administrative staff, headed by Carmen, had become very comfortable organizing the logistics of the conference, as well, so everything went quite smoothly. The yearly national marketing and sales conference had officially become an essential part of our organizational culture. This conference that was started as a means to evaluate a crisis had become a venue to celebrate our successes!

Another opportunity presented itself in May. The Regent fund that had invested in our company some three years earlier suffered significant losses in the Russian capital market and was looking to reduce their involvement in the region. They expressed an interest in selling their investment in our company back to the rest of the shareholders, who were thrilled to retrieve their proportionate interest at a fraction of the selling price. We made a quick deal, and we were back to the original group of shareholders who started the venture.

Once we saw signs of improvement in our performance, Eli raised the concern that our shareholders' loans, the great majority of which were owed to Alan, were very large and continued to grow. Therefore, no matter what we did to increase the value of the enterprise, this additional value would be eaten up by the loans and nothing would be left for the equity holders.

Eli approached Alan about this issue, and Alan soon realized that it would be difficult to keep Eli's interest in the business much longer unless we did something about the present scenario. Alan agreed to restructure the loans in a way that would cap the interest rate retro-actively. That resulted in a significant reduction in the current loans level and slowed down their future growth. Now, all shareholders' interests in the business were once again aligned, and we could focus on generating an increase in value that would benefit all of us.

An interesting advertising opportunity presented itself during the 2000 Summer Olympics in Sydney, Australia. I was watching TV coverage of the games one day and saw a young Romanian swimmer, Diana Mucanu, win two gold medals in the backstroke. I called Eli immediately and shared the idea that we should get her as a spokes-person for one of our brands. He followed up without delay and managed to secure a deal with her agent. Our second wind gave us just the push we needed, because we got the jump on Coke. They tried to get her too but they were too late.

We made Diana Mucanu the spokesperson for Perla. The slogan was a nice play on words between mineral water and her triumphs in the swimming pool:

*We are the Best in Water.*

We kept this wisely selected campaign going successfully for quite a while.

One more development gave us a boost before the year was over. Moldova, a small, land-locked country neighboring Romania, was part of the Soviet Union until its breakup in the 1990s. However, the history of Moldova is a bit more complicated. It had been part of Romania years earlier and was torn out of the country as a result of World War II. The majority of its inhabitants were ethnic Romanians, and the balance were Russians who were planted in the region by Stalin to create a sort of new "reality" that could not be reversed.

After the revolution in Romania and the breakdown of the Soviet Union, Moldova became an independent republic. Many assumed Romania and Moldova would reunite, but the Russian minority had other plans. They did not want to become an even smaller and relatively powerless element in a united Romania, so a civil war looked imminent. The Russian minority relied on the presence of a division of the Russian army that was situated on the eastern border of Moldova to hold their influence and created a separate entity, a semi-autonomous Trans-Dniester Region. Moldova gave up the idea of reuniting with Romania in order to avert war.

Moldova was what PCI called a "white territory." That meant that no Pepsi bottler was present, and therefore there were no sales of its brands in the area. We saw Moldova as an opportunity for expansion. Our VP of sales, Itzick Kutchuk, and the ever-enterprising Moshe Arbel put together a plan to begin selling Pepsi in that market. We received the blessing of Pepsi and found a local beverage company called Vitanta to be our distributor. Vitanta was the leading beer company in Moldova, and we needed a strong distribution company like them to represent us. Coke was already well positioned in Moldova and had a significant head start on Pepsi. The market was too small for us to offset the costs of a production plant or the development of our own distribution, so we decided to export our products from Romania and rely on Vitanta for distribution.

By the end of 2000, we officially felt the benefits of a second wind. The year recorded a solid growth period for all of our brands. Our overall volume grew by close to 25 percent, and the Pepsi brands grew almost 40 percent. We had finally turned the corner on a difficult period and started to perform well once again.

We entered the first year of the millennium energized by the strong performance of 2000. Our budget for 2001 included a meaningful sum for investment for the first time since our crisis years began. One of our upcoming investments was a nonreturnable glass bottling line for our main plant in Bucharest. This represented another first in the field of packaging. A second investment was to create a new warehouse near our Bucharest plant. In addition, we set aside money to invest in a large number of new distribution trucks to replace our aging fleet and new coolers for our retail outlets. This began a multiyear drive to narrow the gap between branded Pepsi coolers and those branded by Coke and European Drinks.

In March, the first true five-star hotel opened in Bucharest—The Marriott Grand Hotel. The Marriott chain searched for a number of years for the right location, and they finally settled on a monstrous structure that Ceausescu built right next to the People's Palace just before the end of his reign. Ceausescu originally intended to use the structure to host guests of the state, and it was built in a very similar style to the People's Palace. It was never quite completed and, for years after the revolution, it stood empty with cranes in and around it as evidence of the abrupt end to the old regime.

The Marriott chain invested a large sum of money to finish it, and held a grand opening. The chairman of Marriott came to visit and announced that it was the nicest hotel in their entire chain.

At that time, Itzick Kutchuk, our VP of sales, asked me to move to the Marriott from the Hilton. The Hilton was a relatively small hotel in the center of the city, and I had been very comfortable there since it opened a few years earlier. However, Itzick had a reason for asking me to move. He had secured an exclusivity beverage contract with the hotel and promised to house our guests there in return.

I hesitated at first. I was very comfortable at the much smaller Hilton. I was getting personal service there, as a frequent guest, and I also liked the location. Among other things, it was right across the street from a beautiful concert hall called the Atheneum. It was quite convenient for me to hop in for concerts there whenever I stayed in the city. I was afraid I would get lost in the gigantic Marriott and the quality of service would not be as high.

Nevertheless, I had to honor our promise. On the upside, the Marriott was less than five minutes from our plant and offices, and that was very convenient. I started to stay at the Marriott, and very quickly felt right at home there. First, the employees were all very service oriented. Their training was exemplary. The unbelievable difference between the Marriott and the early days I spent at the Intercontinental, when guests were a nuisance, did not go by unnoticed.

A second surprise at the Marriott was that the basement of the hotel had the finest health club I have ever experienced in a hotel anywhere in the world! It was spacious, with state-of-the-art equipment and knowledgeable trainers. During the morning hours, it was mostly empty too, so it was heaven to any guest looking to stay in shape on a business trip.

Last but certainly not least, the food was excellent at the Marriott. I particularly enjoyed their northern Italian restaurant, La Cucina. The food was not just wonderful—it was authentic, and the waiters would take a break from tending tables occasionally to sing opera arias! Altogether, the switch to the Marriott was extremely beneficial. The fact that they served our brands in style was not a trivial point either.

In late March, I took my first trip to Moldova. I needed to have a firsthand impression of the market we had just entered a few months earlier. Moshe accompanied me, and our first stop was to pay a visit to Vitanta, our distributor. We toured their production facility and then explored the market in Chisinau, the capital city.

I was pleasantly surprised by what I found in Moldova. I had heard that the country was the "poor relative" of Romania, but I found Chisinau to be clean and the people elegant. In the evening, our host took us to a local restaurant, and the food was very good. I was happily surprised to also see a string quartet playing at the restaurant. The four female musicians were obviously very accomplished musicians. I found out later they were members of the Chisinau Philharmonic. Their monthly income ranged from $20 to $40; they had no choice but to find other ways to supplement their meager salaries.

The next day, we were escorted to a vineyard outside of the city, called Cricova. It was a unique place—entirely underground. The area had been dug out some fifty years earlier so that the limestone could be used for building. They discovered then that it was a perfect location to store wines because of its constant temperature and humidity level, so they decided to create a vineyard there.

There were long tunnels underground that were named after various grape varieties, such as Cabernet Sauvignon, Riesling, etc. They showed us their vast collection of international wines, and I was shocked to find a large selection of Western European wines dating back to the thirties. We were told that it was part of the private collection of the Nazi leader, Herman Gehring. When the Soviets conquered Berlin, they took all sorts of souvenirs back with them, and this wine collection was one of them. The vineyard was made in the fifties, in the latter years of Stalin's rule in the Soviet Union, and Stalin had given one-third of that wine collection to the new vineyard as a gift.

We were treated to a royal wine tasting of the vineyard's brands, accompanied by wonderful food, in one of their magnificent halls. In the ceiling, we could see fossils of fish, evidence of a prehistoric period when that area was covered by the Black Sea. At the end of the wine tasting, we saw picture of famous people who also toured the vineyard over the years. One of them was Yuri Gagarin, the Soviet cosmonaut and first human to travel into space. He was honored for his achievement by a wine tasting here, and they had saved his hand-written note thanking them for the experience. The dates were October 9-10, 1966, which meant that Yuri stayed at the vineyard overnight. This visit to Moldova was eye opening. It showed me that even a poor country could have a rich history with unique and educational points of interest.

May of 2001 marked the tenth anniversary of the EBA, our exclusive license agreement with PCI. It meant that we needed to extend the term of our contract beyond the initial ten years. We had to meet a test in order to do so, which was related to capacity. We had to withstand a technical analysis of the production capacity of all of our bottling lines, and the total had to exceed a certain figure dictated by a formula in the EBA. We had actually had that test done the previous year and passed it with flying colors, and so the extension was granted automatically before the end of the original term.

The year was progressing very nicely. We passed important tests, reached out into new markets, and our sales volumes were up, particularly in the Pepsi brands. Our lower-priced brand, Kick, was on a decline and had become a much smaller portion of our portfolio, but that was actually good news. It signaled the improvement of the economy and increased purchasing power of consumers. They were switching back to A brands.

In August, I was on a family vacation in the Netherlands when I received a dreadful call. Eli's wife, Zohara, phoned me early on Saturday morning with news that shook me to my foundation. Our VP of sales, Itzick, and his wife, Edna, were killed in a car accident the night before. They were on the road to Constanta to celebrate his birthday when their car veered off the road and crashed into a tree. Other members of our management team were traveling with them in other cars, and they witnessed the terrible event. I took an immediate flight to Israel where the bodies would be taken for the funeral. It was an unbearably sad day. Their two daughters were in utter despair, and the tragic event left a huge hole in our organization as well. Itzick was the heart and soul of our sales force, and his sudden departure affected everyone. He would be sorely missed.

On September 11, we gathered for one of our quarterly board meetings. A couple of years earlier, I had changed the quarterly meetings to two in-person meetings and two phone meetings as a cost-cutting measure. This was a phone meeting, so we had people situated in various parts of the world connecting in to the call. Our Romanian counsel, Ion Nestor, Eli, and I were in our offices at the plant in Bucharest; Alan was in his office in New York; Jeff was in Washington, D.C., on a business trip; and Dennis and Shelly were in Louisville, Kentucky.

The meeting started, as usual, at nine o'clock in the morning New York time. A few minutes into the meeting, Alan said that he just heard that a plane hit the Empire State Building, and he commented that there was no reason for that kind of accident on such a beautiful, clear day. Soon afterward, we heard that there was another incident, and we found out that the planes had actually hit the World Trade Center. At that point, it was clear that this was no accident. It was a planned attack.

We cut the meeting short and came out of the office just in time to watch the collapse of the second building live on TV. We were all terribly shaken up by the event that unfolded during our international call. A few days later, we learned that the attack hit even closer to home. One of our secretaries for a number of years, Gabi Iordache, left us to move to the United States and live with an American who had a short stint as a marketing manager with us. She found a job with a company that had offices in the World Trade Center. Gabi was on her way to work that morning, but she was late. When she arrived, the planes had already struck the building, and her life was spared.

In December, we decided to repeat an event we initiated a few years earlier and hold a board meeting in Cyprus. This time we held the meeting in conjunction with Quadgat, the joint venture company in which we owned a majority in partnership with Gat. The Quadgat board handled the affairs of our juice brand Prigat. We stayed at the same lovely resort just outside of the town of Limasol. It was a more intimate group this time, but the atmosphere was no less festive. Some of the Quadgat board members were kibbutzniks, which meant they were part of a socialistic society that historically provided nothing in the way of fringe benefits, even for high-level managers. This was a rare treat for them.

We finished the year once again with very good results. The Pepsi brands grew by over 30 percent, and Prigat and Perla showed very strong numbers. Our profitability was getting healthier every month, and that helped to finance most of our investment needs.

At the beginning of 2002, Antonio notified us that the regional business unit had nominated our operation for the Bottler of the Year award in 2001. This was a sign that we had earned renewed appreciation from the PCI organization. It felt really good to know that our achievements did not go unnoticed. We did not win the award, but we were proud to once again be on the short list of outstanding Pepsi bottlers. Our organization could stand tall.

The budget for 2002 included another very aggressive investment plan. In fact, for the first time we put together a three-year plan that addressed our needs in every aspect of the business. The focus for the current year was twofold: First, we would purchase a significant number of coolers to get a jumpstart on the road to narrow the gap between our competitors and us. Second, we chose to invest in a new computerized system. Our existing data system was outdated and no longer capable of supporting our complex needs.

We chose an internal committee to review offers from various suppliers, and it turned out the best solution came from a company called Wizrom. Eli's wife, Zohara, owned the company, and it had become one of the leading software houses in Romania. Wizrom had come a long way from the early days when they provided us with our very first software package. Eli stayed out of the negotiations process to avoid any issue of a conflict of interest, and the committee reported directly to me.

We reached a very important milestone in 2002: the celebration of our company's tenth anniversary. I felt it was a perfect time to get the board to the location of the company's registered office in the British Virgin Islands. Various members of the board had expressed a desire to have a meeting there one day, and now that our business was once again strong, it was the right time. Flying into the British Virgin Islands was not so easy. Most of the members had to take a complicated route to get there. Eli and I were going with our spouses from Israel, and we had to fly to Madrid, then to Puerto Rico, and then finally to the British Virgin Islands.

When we arrived in Puerto Rico, I realized that I had a small problem. Ever since the September 11 terrorist attacks, the authorities in Puerto Rico required that everyone, even people continuing on to other destinations, clear immigration as if they were staying in the country. Therefore, we needed a visa to the United States, as Puerto Rico was a U.S. territory. Unfortunately, my visa was in an old passport that I had left at home, not expecting to need it. My travel agent did not know about the new regulations, so she never passed the information on to me. I explained my situation to the immigration person and said that I was continuing on to the British Virgin Islands. That person finally agreed to let me continue on, but had a flight attendant accompany me during our short stay and then see me onto the plane.

Once we made it to the British Virgin Islands, I left that incident behind me and enjoyed the place along with everyone else. We stayed at a beautiful resort, toured the island, and took pleasure in some wonderful meals. It was the first time the entire group and their spouses had gotten together in a few years, and it felt like a family reunion. I prepared a special gift for all the board members: a silver-plated pen with an inscription commemorating the event.

At the end of our stay, we parted ways and began our long journeys back home. When we stopped in Puerto Rico, I expected the same routine I experienced on the way to the British Virgin Islands, but I was in for a rude awakening. This time, they separated me from my group and placed me in a segregated area reserved for people awaiting deportation from the country. I stayed there for the entire layover, and then someone accompanied me directly to my plane. I didn't get my passport back until after the plane landed in Madrid. The entire unpleasant experience left a sour taste in my mouth at the end of an otherwise magnificent trip.

In May, it was once again time for our annual marketing and sales conference. Eli created a new concept in order to add to the level of excitement: the Unreasonable Project Competition. Employees from every part of the organization were invited to present unique projects. The criteria included specifying the resources they needed to complete the project as well as the expected outcome; the results had to be out of the ordinary— something that could not be achieved in the normal course of business. The approved projects would be presented at the conference, and the winner would receive the equivalent of one billion lei, which was around $30,000. The winning project would be determined in time for the next conference, based on results that the project achieved throughout the intervening year. We made a statement with this competition: We are no ordinary business looking to achieve ordinary results. Our aspirations are much higher!

In June, we added a new twist to our tale—a Pepsi Twist, that is. It was a simple proposition: a cola soft drink with a twist of lemon already inside. It was expected to be a temporary gimmick to provide a boost for cola sales, but it actually enjoyed decent success in other markets. We introduced the new drink to Romania with a unique marketing campaign. There were live surprises everywhere, like people jumping out of store displays with Pepsi Twist signs. It was a tremendous success, and our sales spiked significantly, allowing us to take additional share of the cola segment. The best part of the campaign was that there was very little cannibalization of our regular cola sales, meaning that it added sales to us at the expense of the competition, not our other cola products. In a relatively short time, our market had one of the largest Pepsi Twist volumes for PCI worldwide!

During the third quarter, we were very pleased to find out that we had won another PCI award: the Regional Innovation Award. We received it in recognition of our continuing efforts to introduce Pepsi brand line extensions, such as additional flavors. Our success with Pepsi Twist was the leading reason for receiving this prestigious award. We were even more pleased to learn that our good friend and supporter, Antonio, won the Regional Franchise Manager of the Year Award. A well-deserved achievement, it was helped along quite a bit by the performance of our operation.

Eli had one overwhelming concern as he started to plan for 2003. Our business was about to finish the third consecutive year of very aggressive growth, and he sensed that many in our organization believed it would be quite difficult to continue this level of performance. Eli looked for a way to build on our momentum and instill in our management the belief that we had even greater opportunities ahead of us.

He discussed his concerns with our strategic organizational consultant, Yigal, and they decided to take the top management team on an outdoor training experience. Yigal teamed up with a group that arranged the activities, and he handled the content. They chose the area of Antalia in the southern part of Turkey as the location.

The day before the trip, we all convened at the plant in Bucharest. Yigal took us through a novel idea called the Winning Concept. It centered around the need of an organization to identify elements that bring it success and find a way to recreate those elements repeatedly and build on their achievements. The entire concept sounded theoretical, and our management group had a hard time relating to it.

Nevertheless, we took a flight to Antalia, and that is where the real experience began. There were ten of us: Eli, our top eight managers, and me. As soon as we arrived in Antalia, we received all sorts of assignments. We were dropped off at a random location and had to find our own way to the hotel by solving a riddle. Later that evening we learned a route on the map, and the next day we had to navigate our way through a rural area without using any maps. We bargained with local residents in the area—who spoke not a word of English— for food and supplies, and later we had to use whatever we managed to obtain to cook ourselves a meal.

Some of the assignments were in small groups and others for the whole group, with one of us assigned the role of group leader. Somewhere during the course of this experience, the Winning Concept started to speak to us. We saw how our performance level increased dramatically when we followed a briefing and debriefing process, looking at how we made decisions and analyzing better ways to make future determinations.

We ended the three-day adventure in the town of Antalia, where we were treated to a Turkish hamam (bath) indulgence and a festive dinner. It was an extremely powerful experience for all ten of us, individually and as a team. We came back reenergized and carrying a strong belief in our ability to succeed. This was the first step on a new journey for our entire organization. Some six layers of management would take part in similar experiences, and the Winning Concept became embedded in our organizational culture.

As always, PCI continued to look for ways to expand its beverage portfolio. In some cases, it would buy additional brands. When that was not possible, PCI would enter into an alliance with attractive brands. This was the case with Lipton Iced Tea. Pepsi secured a broad cooperation agreement with Unilever, the owner of the Lipton brand, which covered a number of countries. When Romania became part of that agreement, we jumped on the opportunity to enter into an additional segment of the market that we felt had a lot of growth potential. We signed a license agreement with Lipton and prepared to start production of the product.

After months of preparation, we went live with our new information system in early December. It significantly improved our data-analysis capabilities and the level of control we had over our remote branches. Essentially, the new system allowed our head office to view online any activity that occurred in any location where the company had a presence. At last, we had launched ourselves into the twenty-first century.

We continued to have discussions at our board meetings about which companies might be interested in acquiring our business. Two strong Pepsi bottlers were active in our region. The first was Pepsi Bottling Group (PBG). It was the largest Pepsi bottler worldwide and was involved in Russia and some of the Balkan countries. The second was PepsiAmericas (PAS). This was Pepsi's second largest bottler. It had taken over the Pepsi operation in Poland, Hungary, and the Czech and Slovak republics a few years earlier.

We felt that PAS would be the natural buyer for our Romanian operation, as it would be a logical expansion for them. However, we had no contact with that organization—that is until the two remaining members of the Kentucky group, Dennis and Shelly, took action. Without consulting anyone, they contacted the manager of PAS in Louisville. He referred them to the chief operating officer, Larry Young, who expressed interest in meeting with us. Just as they had done some twelve years earlier with PCI, their lack of inhibition got us our first meeting with PAS.

We arrived at the end of 2002 having achieved substantial success by catching a second wind. Our volume had grown by 75 percent over the last three years, and our Pepsi volume had grown by 150 percent! We increased the market share of all of our main brands and were once again among the best-performing bottlers of PCI. Most importantly, we believed the best was yet to come.

# CHAPTER 13: SAILING
# WITH FULL FORCE

---

*The meeting of preparation with opportunity gener-
ates the offspring we call luck.*

## —Anthony Robbins

---

In early January of 2003, Eli and I met with Antonio for a brain-
storming session. Antonio was a very close ally by that point,
and we showed him all our cards. We shared our thoughts on every
aspect of our business, because we knew he would respond with
candid feedback and valuable ideas. This session was geared toward
preparation for our presentation to Nish Kankiwala, the head of
PepsiCo Beverages International (PBI) Europe. It would also be our
first meeting with the COO of PAS, Larry Young.

We put quite a bit of thought into the upcoming meeting. It was
important to make the best first impression possible, and we needed
to present a coherent message about our intentions. One of the essential points we wanted to get across was a complete alignment

between Eli and me and a clear mandate from our shareholders. We thought through every possible angle, even going through mock question-and-answer sessions, analyzing the company's opportunities and threats, and setting clear objectives for the meeting.

Finally, the day of the presentation arrived. It took place in PBI's office in Richmond, outside of London. Eli and I gave a detailed presentation that covered a synopsis of the company and our market, highlights of the last three years of performance, and our plan for the coming year. It went quite well, and everyone congratulated us. Our careful preparation bore fruit, and we established the foundation for a dialogue with PAS.

When I returned home, I found an e-mail announcement about a PAS press conference that would be held on the Internet. I checked my watch and found out it was just about to start! I quickly signed in and listened to the conference. The chairman of PAS, Bob Pohlad, spoke about the international side of their business and plans for expansion, among other things. It felt like an ominous sign. Had they already included Romania in their plans for international expansion?

At the end of January, Antonio notified us that we were once again nominated for PBI's 2002 bottler of the year award. We were filled with gratitude when we had a chance to look over the form that was filed by the European business unit. It spelled out our achievements, volume growth, market share gain, and other usual milestones. But this time a very important word was added—sustainability. They believed our strong performance had every chance of continuing.

We did not win the award that year. It went to China. However, we were very pleased to be nominated two years in a row for the prestigious honor. It meant we were clearly on the radar screen of the top management at PBI.

In early March, we received an exciting note from Larry Young. It stated that PepsiAmericas was indeed interested in acquiring our company. Larry indicated a range of values for the operation based on an EBITDA (Earnings Before Interest, Taxes, Depreciation, and Amortization) multiple—a widely accepted form for valuation of a business. He said that if this range was acceptable to our shareholders, PAS was ready to move quickly on finalizing a transaction. We conferred with the shareholding group and gave a positive answer. Then, we set up dates for Larry to visit our operation the following month. The visit went very well, and we could feel momentum building. At the end of Larry's visit, we extended an invitation to PAS to attend our upcoming annual marketing and sales conference.

The conference was scheduled to take place in early May. Eli planned to take the Winning Concept that was introduced to our top management team at the outdoor training experience the previous fall and share it with the entire sales organization. He did it in dramatic fashion, making a lasting impression on everyone in attendance:

One by one, three large boxes were brought on stage. The first box said, "creating the opportunity"; the second box, "actualizing the opportunity"; and the third, "keeping the momentum." At the end, Eli walked on stage and turned the boxes to form the word *Winners!* And so that was the main theme of the conference, and the rest of the time was spent on discussing and explaining in more detail exactly what that meant.

We also used the conference as a venue to introduce new products that we were about to launch. The main product introduction for that year was Mountain Dew. It was the fastest-growing carbonated soft drink in the United States, and we felt it could add strength to our own CSD portfolio. It was also going to make one of our shareholders extremely happy. Shelly had been trying for some time to convince us to introduce that product.

PAS had accepted our invitation, and they sent Mike Holmes, one of their senior executives with significant regional experience, to attend. We could sense that the highly charged atmosphere of the conference made quite an impression on him.

Just days after the conference, we received a draft letter of intent from PAS to purchase our operation. The terms were spelled out in detail, and while we had a number of issues with the offer, we felt that the process was gaining force. For the first time in our company's history, we had a serious suitor for our business.

We began to share information with PAS on our business and engaged in an active dialogue regarding the prospect of a sale. One of our major concerns was the issue of confidentiality. We felt it was premature to share this process with our management, as it could have a disruptive and negative effect on motivation and performance. We needed to have a bit more certainty that the transaction was actually going to take place before we "went public" with the news.

As I became more and more confident in the eventuality of a sale, I started to prepare something special for Eli to commemorate the event. I found a portrait of Frank Sinatra on the Internet called "The Voice," by LeRoy Neiman and thought it would be the perfect gift for an avid Sinatra fan like Eli. I contacted the gallery in New York that dealt with Neiman Marcus's works, purchased a serigraph of the painting, and arranged for it to be sent to Israel.

The June board meeting was to be in Romania, as usual. This time we found a golf resort about two hours from Bucharest to hold the assembly. It was the very first such resort in Romania. Many of our board members were active golfers, and we knew they would enjoy the place. For those who were not golfers, we arranged lessons so that everyone could take an active part.

There was one other very special element to this meeting, a personal one for me. Shelly was a tenor saxophone player, and he had been trying for a long time to find a way for us to play together. Unfortunately, we knew of no music that was written for saxophone and French horn. That did not dissuade Shelly. He decided we had to make it happen. He hired an arranger to write an arrangement for our two instruments for a few well-known tunes. Then Shelly asked me to arrange a rental saxophone for him and to bring my horn. We rented a sax at a local conservatory, and I brought the spare horn I kept at the office in Bucharest. We had little time to rehearse, but on the second day of the event, we gave a short concert in front of the board members and top management. This "show" added a very special touch to the festivities, and we repeated the performance in the cafeteria at the Bucharest plant in front of a large number of our employees. The audiences seemed to appreciate both of our performances, and we enjoyed a chance to finally play together.

On July 17, after much discussion and debate, we signed a letter of intent with PAS for the sale of our company. This allowed PAS to start their involved due diligence process. As a large enterprise in the beverage industry, they had gone through many such endeavors, so they had a well-structured process of action. It called for quite a number of people from every discipline relevant to our business to come and inspect our operation. PAS sent us a template that detailed the schedule of who was coming and when over the course of eight weeks. This put a tremendous burden on our management, especially on our financial team, led by Leon, who by this time was our CFO. They had to cope with their routine tasks and at the same time be responsive to a request for a large amount of information.

Obviously, at this point we had to tell our top management something about the development, because they were going to be involved in the process and would be hosting many of the visitors. We agreed that for the time being we would describe it as PAS exploring the possibility of a strategic investment in our business. There was no guarantee that the process would end in a sale, so it was very important for us to create as few waves as possible. We needed to minimize the anxiety level regarding a change of ownership. A potential investment from a strong bottler was a lot less threatening than a complete transfer of power.

This is when we were introduced to John Bierbaum, a close aide to the chairman of PAS, Bob Pohlad. He would be negotiating the next phase of the transaction with us. We had expected to continue to deal with Larry Young, with whom we signed the letter of intent, but it turned out that in a large organization like PAS, every person had a separate responsibility. Once we had gotten beyond a letter of intent, we were handed over to John. We had no choice but to deal with the negotiator PAS designated for this new stage of the transaction.

Our performance in the first nine months of 2003 was incredible. Pepsi volume was up by over 40 percent. We could see our diligence and preparation for success starting to pay off enormously. This is why PBI chose not to wait until the end of the year to reward us. Antonio came up with the idea that PBI would sponsor a weekend retreat for our top management in Tuscany to show their appreciation for a job well done. I loved the idea. There was no better reward than spending time in one of the most famous wine-producing regions of the world. Antonio assembled a program that combined visits to interesting sights in the area and opportunities to taste great wines at a number of wineries.

The trip commenced in early November when Eli, our top management, and I took a flight to Milan. From there we traveled by bus down to Florence and spent some time touring that great city. Next, we traveled to the small vineyard of Borgo San Felice and participated in a wine tasting. We then had a typical Tuscan dinner and spent the night at the inn that was part of the vineyard grounds.

In the morning, we visited Sienna and then drove to Montalcino, the village where the great wine Brunello di Montalcino is produced. We had a wonderful wine tasting at Castello Banfi and lunch at the vineyard accompanied by their impressive wines.

In the afternoon, we visited San Giminiano and ended up at Villa San Luchese for dinner and overnight accommodations. It was a unique evening, as some of us got up in the middle of the night to witness a total eclipse of the moon. When the Earth passed between the sun and the moon, it was breathtaking to see the moon become totally dark, with just a single ring around it.

The next day we traveled to a town on the coast called Viareggio, where we had lunch and then began our journey home. It was a fabulous weekend—a fine reward for the continued top-notch performance of our senior management.

Unfortunately, we came back from our weekend to find our discussions with PAS had hit a snag. They had completed the due diligence process and found most everything to be in order, but they had one major concern. The letter of intent called for the price to be based on a multiple of EBITDA. Our performance was improving each month, and they realized that if that trend continued, the ultimate price would be much higher than they had anticipated. This raised a concern about the sustainability of our results. PAS was not convinced that our very strong performance could be continued in the future.

One of their related concerns was the recent strength of the Romanian currency. They felt that it had an unusually positive effect on our financial results. We traded long e-mails with John on this subject and eventually met face-to-face with him in New York in mid-December, at the time of our board meeting. We tried to look for creative ways to address his concern, but we finally acknowledged that there was a wide gap in our respective views on the valuation of the business, even though the mechanism for that valuation had long been established.

Regardless of our problems with PAS, 2003 ended on a high note with outstanding performance results. Our total volume grew by almost 35 percent, and the volume of our Pepsi brand grew over 50 percent! The recent years of aggressive growth allowed us to finally reach the level we achieved in 1995, which had been our high mark to that point.

At the beginning of 2004, we continued our trend of strong sales performance, but we began to look for new ways to enhance our business. One potential move was to incorporate PepsiCo's other line of business, salty snack foods. PepsiCo was best known for its beverage brands, but FritoLay, its snack food division, had always been an important part of the overall business. It was surprising for us to learn that PepsiCo was a much stronger player in snack foods—clearly the worldwide leader in salty snacks.

For most of its history, PepsiCo managed these two businesses totally separately, but recently they had come to the conclusion that there was a way to leverage the two sides of their business. They developed a concept called "The Power of One" that spelled out the benefits of jointly pushing these businesses in the marketplace. We felt strongly that our market was a good candidate to put this concept into action. Naturally, Eli and I discussed it with Antonio, and he agreed that we should look for opportunities to promote the joint business. Our first step was to initiate a dialogue with FritoLay.

February 10 was our first meeting with the regional manager of FritoLay in Bucharest. It was a memorable day, but not in the way we imagined. When I got back to my office after that meeting, I had an e-mail message from Dennis. The subject line read, "Very sad news." It went on to say that Shelly had passed away that morning. His heart had been weakened by a variety of problems over the years, and it finally gave in. It was indeed very sad. As I wrote in a eulogy that went to all of our employees, Shelly was one of the originators of the idea of our business in Romania. He had always kept a keen interest in the business, was excited about every development, and was very supportive of our efforts. We could take heart in the knowledge that he lived to see his idea become a thriving business. On a personal note, I was happy that we had also managed to fulfill his desire to perform musically together a year earlier. Our friend and partner would be dearly missed.

Later that month, Eli and I participated in a PBI event called "The Sales Leadership Forum." This event celebrated individual salespeople from various markets who made a unique contribution to the success of the Pepsi brands. Two representatives of our own sales organization were invited to participate, and Eli and I came to show our appreciation for their achievements. One of our two representatives was chosen at this forum to represent the European business unit in a worldwide event to be held later that year in the United States. Indeed, it was yet another exciting point of recognition for our organization.

Meanwhile, our discussions with PAS were going nowhere. While we continued to look for innovative ways to handle our differences, it was clear that PAS was unable to come to terms with the issue of sustainability. Our strong performance turned out to be the stumbling block in the negotiations. Some members of our team suggested that we approach PAS with our "bottom line price" and see if they would accept it. I was strongly opposed to that approach. Our business had performed extremely well for an extended period, and we were still on a strong upward trend. There was absolutely no reason for us to sell ourselves short.

John notified us in early March that the letter of intent, which had already lapsed, was no longer valid, and PAS did not plan to continue discussions. It was a disappointing end to an arduous process that had started some fourteen months earlier, but the conclusion was unavoidable. We didn't waste any time mourning the lost opportunity. We had a business to run, and we focused on its success. I decided not to delay the present I prepared for Eli, and I gave him the Frank Sinatra serigraph. He deserved it irrespective of whether or not we were able to conclude a deal with PAS.

We received some further good news from PBI at around the same time. Our main production plant in Bucharest had received the bronze quality award for its performance in 2003. Antonio said in his announcement to us that this "completed the picture." Our operation had surpassed every key performance indicator (KPI) in recent years. We were quite pleased with the award, but Eli and I still had our eyes on some more prestigious PBI awards we had not yet won. We were sailing with full force and had no intention of slowing our pace.

April of 2004 brought a very interesting session for our entire management team: a professional music conductor explained to us the inner workings of leading an orchestra. The point was to convey the idea that managing a business is like conducting an orchestra. One needs to unite a number of different elements and bring out the best in each of them for the total enterprise to reach a premium performance level. As a lifelong amateur musician, I found the message particularly powerful. I shared with the audience my experience that an orchestra is only as good as its worst musician. The same is true for a business and its management team. At the end of the session, the National Radio Orchestra assembled, and various people from our group had an opportunity to try to conduct them. The exercise provided a concrete message about the challenges involved with leadership, and we all took something away from the experience.

Our annual marketing and sales conference took place in May that year, and we changed the venue to a location on the Black Sea coast. We built on the concept of *Teamwork* and conducted all sorts of activities in groups. As the assignments were carried out, there was an element of competition among the groups; at the same time, we felt a strong sense of overall cooperation.

The Unreasonable Project Competition had become a tradition, and Eli took it a little further in 2004. He initiated a company-wide unreasonable challenge: if the company managed to surpass $100 million in turnover (over 40 percent growth over the previous year), then a $1 million bonus would be shared by all employees. This powerful message went beyond the sales organization to our entire workforce and gave every single employee the incentive to stretch our company's performance to its limits.

The final assignment of the conference was one in which everyone took part. We spelled out our brand name—Pepsi—on the beach using all three hundred people in attendance. One team managed the affair from a high point on the beach where they could see the entire group, and the whole exercise was videotaped. We even joked about contacting the Guinness Book of World Records to observe our event; in any case, it helped us to end the conference on a high note and send everyone to their respective destinations with renewed energy and excitement.

Eli and I took that energy directly to FritoLay. We paid a visit to their operation in Greece to further our efforts regarding a possible relationship with the snack food side of PepsiCo. It was interesting to see a production plant that was quite different from the bottling operations with which we had become so familiar over the years. The distribution side of the business was similar, though, which was one of the reasons why PepsiCo initiated the concept of the "Power of One."

As a side note, the trip to visit FritoLay put us in Athens just a few months before the Summer Olympics. We observed that the place looked far from ready for the big event, and the locals we met projected a major failure. No one was optimistic about everything coming together in time. We were pleasantly surprised when the Olympic Games turned out to be a huge success in spite of their grim projections.

We chose Covasna as the venue for our June board meeting, as it was the location of our new mineral water factory. Perla had been a mineral water brand in our portfolio for a number of years, but the main problem with that brand was that we did not own the source of the water. We were a tenant of another brand of mineral water, and our destiny was at their mercy. We needed our own source so that we could invest in a brand for the long term.

We assigned Ioan the task of finding such a source, and after an extensive search, he came to the area of Covasna, which was about three hours north of Bucharest. We tested the water and arrived at the conclusion that it was of very high quality. The problem was that it was in the middle of nowhere. It was a "green field" operation in the truest sense.

In spite of the remote location, we acquired some land and put together a plan to build a factory in the area. Mineral water would be the main element, but we also planned to produce some of the other beverages in our portfolio at the new plant. We made all the necessary preparations: purchasing a bottling line and related equipment, getting approval for producing mineral water out of that local source, and finally coming up with a name.

Our marketing department and our ad agency put in a fair amount of work and came up with the name Roua Muntilor—"Mountain Dew" in Romanian. That caused a problem with PepsiCo, who considered it a trademark infringement on their carbonated soft drink.

Eventually, we settled on the shortened name "Roua." We chose to wait until the board meeting to officially inaugurate the new plant.

Eli came up with the idea that we should dedicate the factory to Shelly and name it after him, and everyone enthusiastically accepted the suggestion. The trip to the plant was not so easy, because part of the route was on unpaved roads. Nevertheless, the official ceremony to unveil the factory was a substantial and emotional moment. Shelly's wife, Denise, did the honors and unveiled the sign: "The Sheldon B. Schiller Water Factory." Sadness tinged our joy given the loss of our dear friend, but we all knew that Shelly would be very proud of this development.

At the end of June, Eli and I jumped on an opportunity to meet the new head of the regional PBI business unit, Zein Abdalla, at a PBI gathering of franchises in Amsterdam. We knew it was important to keep in close contact with the top PBI people if we wanted to remain in their scope of vision. We were surprised and honored to be treated to a private lunch with Mr. Abdalla at that time. Our franchise was gaining importance within PBI, and we greatly appreciated the recognition.

An interesting financial development also took place that summer. Our main bank was Alpha Bank of Greece, and Evangelos Kalamakis, a senior officer with the local branch in Bucharest, approached us with a unique proposition. He pointed out that our total debt was quite low relative to our profitability, which we knew was quite true. It had been our business philosophy from the very beginning to rely on an internal generation of cash flow and borrow conservatively.

Evangelos made what seemed like a radical suggestion: he offered a generous long-term loan from the bank that would allow our shareholders to take out most of the proceeds as repayment of their loans. I was quite hesitant at first. This would represent a major shift in the way we had been conducting our financial affairs. It seemed risky. On the other hand, it was an opportunity for our shareholders to have some liquidity in an investment they had been involved in for over twelve years. Eli and I calculated the level of a loan we could afford while still maintaining a reasonable ratio of total debt to our annual cash flow, and we agreed to take the proposition to the board.

Eli's fiftieth birthday arrived in September, and he planned to celebrate it in style. And what would be an appropriate theme for his party? Frank Sinatra, of course! He invited the entire board of directors to come to Israel, and we would hold our first ever board meeting there. Everyone gladly accepted the invitation, and board members came from all over the United States and Europe for his celebration. Eli put a lot of research into the affair and shared with us some unique video clips of his favorite celebrity at the event. We then took the group on a trip to the northern part of the country to view some interesting tourist sites. We spent the night at a boutique hotel called Villa Galilee near the ancient town of Zefat, where we also conducted our board meeting and enjoyed a festive dinner.

At the business portion of the meeting, I had a proposition for the board: we needed to put some serious effort into finding a suitable exit strategy. We had been toying with the idea for some time, and now that discussions with PAS had ended with no positive results, I felt that we needed to engage in a systematic effort to find more than one option for the sale of our business. I had recently come across a new entity called MG Equity. One of its founders, Amir Raveh, was a distant relative of mine. I found out that they had very good contacts in the capital markets in the United Kingdom, and so I asked the board to give them authorization to look for an investment banker for us that would attempt to find investors interested in our company. I admitted that this was a gamble. The company was very young and had limited experience. Nevertheless, I felt we were risking little since they completely based their modest fee request on success. The board gave me the green light, and we launched a radical new attempt at finding some liquidity for our shareholders.

In early October, we embarked on our second outdoor management training excursion. The first event in Turkey was so successful that Eli decided to take the top management through another exercise. This time the venue was Piraeus, Greece. Our mission: to learn how to sail. We spent a couple of days on a yacht, and once again, we completed assignments in small groups and as an entire team. It was a great success and brought our management team even closer together. At the end of the training session, we spent an entire day and a half in strategic planning sessions to tweak the three-year plan we put together the previous year. This ongoing collaboration and preparation was paving the way for future success, and we felt it.

MG Equity put together an event later that month in London, and Eli and I traveled there to participate. They geared it toward introducing companies seeking investment to potential investors and investment bankers. We used that opportunity to meet a few investment bankers MG Equity thought would be suitable to lead the effort for our company. One of those entities was Altium, a midsized investment bank that had some experience in Eastern Europe but had not yet ventured into Romania. We immediately liked their team, led by Stephen Georgiadis. After this event, we received a number of offers for representation, but we had a gut feeling that Altium was the right choice.

Our negotiations with PAS actually bore some fruit during this year as well, even though it didn't result in a sale. The due diligence work performed by PAS alerted us to an issue that we decided to address in 2004. PAS had a problem with the minority interest held by Gat on the juice side of our operation. They did not like the fact that they would end up with a partner in one important segment of the market if they were to acquire our business, and their concerns were legitimate. We decided to address this issue in a unique fashion: we offered Gat a smaller interest in our entire operation in exchange for their interest in the juice business. It was an opportunity for them to become a shareholder in the holding group. That solution would look good to a potential buyer, because they would be buying Gat's interest along with the rest of the shareholders' and would not be stuck with a minority shareholder. The proposition was also appealing to

Gat, because they realized they would be cashing in their interest at the same time and to the same extent as we would. We immediately began a negotiation process to determine the specifics.

Surprisingly, a dialogue with PAS resurfaced toward the end of the year. The first message came from Zein, the head of PBI Europe. He told us he had a conversation with PAS's worldwide COO, Ken Keiser, who expressed an interest in "taking another look" at investing in our company. Shortly thereafter, Ken called Alan to find out if we were still open to a dialogue. Based on our prior internal discussions, Alan introduced the idea of PAS becoming a minority investor first. That would reduce the size of their initial investment and allow them to grow more comfortable with our operation. Both sides liked the idea, so I followed up with Ken, and he suggested I meet with Alex Ware, their executive vice president for business development. We set up a meeting for shortly after the New Year. Our journey was never without a surprising turn or two, and the coming year held an interesting mix of new opportunities.

That brought us to the end of another great year. Our volume was up another 30 percent, and our profitability increased dramatically. All our employees celebrated when turnover surpassed the $100 million mark, warranting the $1 million bonus promised at the sales and marketing conference. On top of that, we had an offer from our principal banker that would allow our shareholders to take some money out, and we were about to recommence discussions with PAS. We had established a new approach to an exit strategy and found the right partner to help us through that process. We felt like we were creating our own luck and sailing with full force into a very promising future. Things were looking pretty good.

# CHAPTER 14: BRINGING THE SHIP HOME

---

*By prevailing over all obstacles and distractions, one may unfailingly arrive at his chosen goal or destination.*

**—Christopher Columbus**

---

After successfully navigating unpredictable waters, we had our destination in sight by 2005. It was time to bring the ship home. The year started with a barrage of activities. In the first few days of the New Year, I met with Alex Ware in London. It was the first meeting in our second round of talks with PAS, and I was somewhat apprehensive about the outcome.

My apprehension quickly evaporated. Alex was my kind of negotiating partner: to the point, solution oriented, and cooperative. We had a very good session and established some important guidelines and follow-up steps. We even managed to attend an exciting Chelsea soccer match—a first for Alex.

Later that month, the top two PepsiCo executives in Europe visited us: Marco Jesi, the overall head of snack food and beverages for PepsiCo Europe, and Zein Abdalla, the head of beverages. This was a very important visit, because it signaled the increasing importance of our operation in PI, and it allowed us to demonstrate the strength of our business. Both executives walked away with a very positive image of our organization.

At the tail end of that visit, we met with the Altium team. They wanted to see our business firsthand before commencing the project of raising capital for the company. We officially signed their engagement letter during that visit. In addition to the commercial terms, which we had agreed on previously, there was a question about the status of our relationship with PAS. We were quite open with Altium about the prospect of an investment by PAS in our company, which, if it materialized, would make their efforts superfluous. We had learned the importance of having a second option, and I felt it was critical to keep Altium committed to this project until the very end. Therefore, I convinced our board to accept a clause in the agreement that stated that Altium would be entitled to the same fee whether we got an investment through their efforts or completed a deal with PAS. This way they would be indifferent to which route we ended up pursuing and would not relax their efforts to get us to a successful conclusion.

In early February, we had a follow-up meeting with PAS in London. This time they brought a whole delegation of people, headed by Ken Keiser, their worldwide COO. The delegation included representatives of different disciplines within the organization, and it was starting to look like they were more committed to the negotiation process this time.

Shortly after that meeting, Antonio notified us that our operation had been nominated for a very prestigious award at PepsiCo: The Donald M. Kendall Co-Founders (DMK) Award. The award was named after the legendary founder of PepsiCo, and was given out each year to outstanding Pepsi bottlers and snack food operators in a variety of categories, based on a three-year performance review. We were asked to give a presentation at an event the following month on Marco Island in Florida. There were very clear guidelines about what the presentation should cover—and one strict rule—the presentation could not exceed twenty minutes!

Antonio, Eli, and I jumped on the assignment, with the help of Eusediu, our marketing director. We eventually concluded that the only way to ensure that we would not exceed the time limit would be to have a "running" presentation. In other words, we set the slides on autopilot with no way to stop them. That forced us to stick to the text and the time allotted to each slide. It also required a generous amount of practice time, which we did not have. The rehearsals included a complex video conference between Milan, Bucharest, and Tel Aviv, as none of us was in the same location. This was very helpful and allowed us to identify the areas where we needed improvement.

Eli and I took the long trip to Marco Island in early March. The route was Tel Aviv to London to Miami to Naples, Florida (on a tiny, six-seat plane), to Marco Island. In whole, the journey took close to twenty-four hours.

Alex and I were making good progress in our discussions with PAS at this time. We were at a point of drafting a new letter of intent (LOI), so we decided to use the opportunity of our trip to the United States for an all-hands-on-deck meeting. Ken from PAS attended, and Alan was also there on our side. A good meeting, it set the tone for an expedited process of negotiation.

After that meeting, Eli and I focused on our main purpose for traveling to the United States: the DMK Award. Our presentation was unique. We took a team approach. Two of us shared the podium, each covering different elements of our market and operation. It was a true testament to the way we shared responsibility for the business. We started with a quick description of our market and then shared our vision statement, which Eli had put together upon his return a few years earlier. The statement read: "Determination for success for the benefit of our Consumers, Customers, Employees, Suppliers, and Shareholders." Our values: "Winners, Entrepreneurial, Innovative, Unreasonable, Responsible corporate citizens, Acting like a respectful family."

Next, we covered highlights of our last three years of performance: *tripling* the volume of our Pepsi brands; nearly doubling our cola market share to bring it to over 30 percent; and improving all key performance indicators (KPIs) for Pepsi, bringing them close to the level of Coke. We topped off the presentation with a three-minute video called *How the Black Sea Was Won*. It demonstrated that with a dedicated effort we could overtake Coke in the market. We concluded right at the twenty-minute mark!

Our presentation scored rave reviews, not only from the panel of judges, but also from people in the audience—including some of our competitors for the prize. Finally, we were able to relax and enjoy the wonderful setting of the event and some of the activities offered to the participants.

The culmination of the entire occasion was a festive dinner where the winners would be announced. Eli and I experienced a rare treat at the cocktail party that preceded the dinner—we met the real Don Kendall in person. He was in his eighties, had a remarkably clear mind, and was happy to share with us the story of how he personally established the roots of the Pepsi business in Romania forty years earlier. He told us that he had been following our performance and was proud of our achievements. The meeting closed a circle in a unique way for all three of us.

At the dinner, we were disappointed to learn that the award in our category (small developing markets) went to Vietnam. We felt the decision was not purely merit based, but our continued presence at the top of Pepsi's list of exceptional performers could not be denied.

A few days after this exhilarating event, we managed to close the term loan with Alpha Bank. For the first time since we started the business, we were able to distribute meaningful funds to our shareholders. It solidified our relationship with the bank and particularly our key counterpart there, Evangelos. The transaction was also one more tribute to the strength of our business.

In late March, Alex and I completed the LOI after only three in-person meetings. The deal we agreed on had two phases: in the first phase, PAS would purchase 49 percent of the company and become a strategic investor; the second phase detailed the future acquisition of the balance of 51 percent ownership. This meant that PAS was given a "call" right (to acquire the 51 percent), and our side had a "put" right (for the sale of that interest), commencing at a future date following the initial investment.

The deal also allowed the existing shareholders to declare a large dividend prior to the closing of the transaction, which would be funded by a new bank loan. The structure was designed to minimize the initial investment by PAS and still allow our shareholders the opportunity to realize significant value. It also created a mechanism to ultimately transfer full ownership to PAS, as neither side wanted to be stuck in the initial position. Upon signing the letter of intent, PAS engaged in an expedited onsite due diligence process, which benefited from the involved process they had gone through just eighteen months earlier.

Our negotiations with PAS were progressing very nicely, and we seemed to be headed for a transaction with them. Nevertheless, Altium continued its efforts to generate financial investors for our company. We engaged in that process with equal seriousness and in parallel to our conversations with PAS—remaining true to our belief that having a second viable option was critical. In fact, we received a few genuine, credible offers through Altium's efforts. A few of those potential investors visited us, and we went through the entire process of showing them our operation. I was committed to maintaining this parallel path until we closed the deal with PAS.

Our annual Marketing and Sales Conference was held in early April, and the theme that year was "Enjoy the Success AND Dare for More." The second part of the theme echoed Pepsi's new slogan. The event was not only a well-guarded tradition and the focal point of our company activities, but it was also drawing attention outside of our organization. Top bottling managers had heard about it and were interested in participating as guests. Therefore, our 2005 conference included guests from PI (including Antonio), representatives from PAS, a Portuguese bottler, and an Israeli bottler. The last two guests were not strangers. They were under Antonio's area of responsibility, and we had gotten to know them over the years. All visitors came out of the experience quite impressed by the high level of energy and special atmosphere that was generated.

One tradition that we initiated at these conferences was to reward employees who had been with the company for ten years. We invited them on stage individually and gave them a special watch as a gift. The only problem was that the list of employees who qualified for this honor got larger every year. By 2005, we had to hold an entirely separate event for over forty of our employees who passed the ten-year mark. This incredible level of loyalty that had developed was a great source of joy. Many of them had stayed with us for a good part of their careers.

Later that month we had to walk through the capacity check that was specified in the EBA with PepsiCo. This was a requirement for the renewal of our license agreement the following year. We had added significant capacity over the previous three years, so it was an easy test to meet. The results secured our automatic renewal for five years starting in May of 2006.

A couple of years earlier we had a PI-sponsored incentive trip to Tuscany for our top management. We continued that tradition in 2005 with a trip to the Algarve region of Portugal. The main purpose of the excursion was for the members of our management team and their spouses to have fun, and we certainly attained that goal. Everyone enjoyed the beautiful area, the resort, and the sumptuous meals. We ended the trip in Lisbon and could not pass on the opportunity to visit the Pepsi bottling plant there. It was just a few weeks after their owner had attended our Sales and Marketing Conference, so we enjoyed the chance to sustain that contact.

Another arena where we were generating a fair amount of success was in advertising. We were restricted to the use of PepsiCo-created campaigns and materials for our Pepsi brands, but we had the freedom to create our own campaigns for Prigat. Leo Burnett was our advertising agency for Prigat, and the creative director, Bogdan Naumovici, took the lead. They did an outstanding job for us and won the Advertising Campaign of the Year Award that year at Ad'Or, an international advertising competition. Leo Burnett also took the Agency of the Year Award for the third time!

We were becoming a company of traditions, and our tradition of holding the June board meeting in Romania became even more special because we chose the Danube Delta as the venue that year. I thought that our board members should experience the natural wonder that I had enjoyed a few years earlier. Our special guests were Josef Schmidt and his wife, Sylvia. Josef had been the Pepsi manager for our market when we started our operation. For the first time, the children of board members were also invited to attend, and our three boys joyfully came along.

The main topic of discussion at the meeting was, of course, the status of our transaction with PAS. There was one item that carried an important personal significance for me: in anticipation of PAS becoming a strategic investor in the company and appointing additional members to the board, the board, at Alan's suggestion, elected me as chairman. With their decision I regained the position I held in the early days of our journey. I had lost my place at the helm during the crisis years, and now it felt like I received a well-earned redemption.

Immediately following the board meeting, we worked feverishly to complete the Gat transaction and make Gat an investor in the entire business, rather than just the juice segment. We also put in an immense amount of work on the PAS transaction. Jeff was working around the clock to navigate the complex documentation that was needed, especially for the deal with PAS. The Gat transaction closed first, as it was a prerequisite for the deal with PAS. Finally, on June 15, we closed with PAS. It was a joyous moment for everyone involved. A most appropriate note arrived from Antonio to commemorate the event:

*This is the completion of one journey and the start of a new one.*

Suddenly, the rewards for all our hard work started to come in a continuous flow. Our drive for excellence in all areas of operation was paying off. In the summer, we scored our first "blue" (the highest level possible) in PI's production quality review. Only a small number of Pepsi plants could boast this prestigious ranking.

In September, we held our first board meeting with the newly appointed PAS members in New York. It included a festive dinner at the 21 Club, one of the best-known culinary institutions in New York. The location was fitting for this very special occasion that marked the beginning of a new journey together.

We were pleased later that fall to receive one additional point of recognition. The local financial magazine, *Capital*, ranked us among the fifty best companies to work for in 2005. The criteria were working conditions, quality of internal cooperation, compensation level, and opportunities for growth. Our company was number four on the list! I can hardly describe how gratifying it was to receive recognition for the way we treated our employees. We had paid careful attention to that as we built our business, and it meant a lot to receive praise for lifting up our employees and their talents.

As part of our annual budget process, we held a strategic planning session in the resort town of Predeal. In the past, our sessions mapped out one year at a time, but by now, we were producing three-year plans. We also had a new issue to resolve, the location of our main plant. The original plant that had served our company since inception was situated in the dead center of Bucharest. Unfortunately, it had become increasingly difficult to operate a production plant from this location. The authorities did not like large distribution trucks roaming the streets of the capital, and the value of real estate in the center of Bucharest had increased to the point that it would be wise to relocate the plant and cash in on the value of the existing location. This was no simple task. It sparked lengthy debates at our session about when, where, and how to move. Of course, we also involved our new strategic investor in these sessions and welcomed their input.

We closed a new loan with Alpha Bank in October, which enabled us to pay the dividends declared prior to the transaction with PAS. With that move, we completed the first phase of our deal with PAS—a process we had started one year earlier at the board meeting in Israel.

The year 2005 turned out to be a significant point in our journey. We had obtained momentous goals, particularly in our relationship with PAS, and it was another banner year for company performance. Our Pepsi volume grew at a pace three times that of Coke. We were happy to learn that our volume level put us into the top thirty Pepsi bottlers worldwide.

Dramatic news appeared in media around the world at the start of 2006: for the first time in 112 years, the market value of PepsiCo exceeded that of the Coca-Cola Company. The gap in the relative value of these two enterprises had been quite wide just a few years earlier. It was the direct result of the increased level of confidence shareholders had in the way PepsiCo was handling its business and the reverse for Pepsi's rival. We felt it was a very ominous sign for Coke brands in our market.

Just when we thought it couldn't get any better, Eli and I received personal letters from Mike White, the CEO of PI, in mid-February. We had been named Bottler of the Year for Europe in 2005, and we were nominated for the worldwide Bottler of the Year Award. In addition, we were nominated once again for the Don Kendall (DMK) Co-Founders Award. So we were up for both of PepsiCo's top awards—one looking at achievements in a single year, and the other for a three-year period. The circle of winners was getting smaller. There were four candidates worldwide for the Bottler of the Year Award and twelve candidates in four categories for the DMK Award. We dared to dream once again of capturing these prestigious awards.

The event itself took place in Paris in late March. This time the presentation for the DMK Award was reserved for PI's executives, so Antonio was given the burden of preparations, and Eli and I were able to relax and enjoy our time in Paris with our spouses. The award ceremony took place at a majestic hall in the famous historic monument, Les Invalides. All of the top people at PepsiCo attended: Don Kendall, Steve Reinemund (the chairman of PepsiCo), and Mike White. Our company was one of only two bottlers that were nominated for both awards. Each of the four candidates for the Bottler of the Year Award was asked to come on stage and receive its regional award, and the full story of their achievements was shared with the audience.

We did not win either award. The DMK Award went to Vietnam for the second year in a row, and the Bottler of the Year Award went to Venezuela. Nevertheless, we walked away from the event with our heads held high. Our organization was among the "crème de la crème" of Pepsi International.

On May 1, we received official notice that PAS was exercising their call right on the balance of the company ownership. It was the earliest possible time for them to do so, according to our agreement. In fact, we had a heated debate over when exactly that "earliest time" fell. The price was based on a multiple of earnings, and given that our profitability was improving each month, it was in the interest of PAS to do it as soon as possible. Our shareholders, on the other hand, wanted to keep the clock ticking just a bit longer. Once we agreed on a date, they sent us an official notice. That meant we had to share the news with our employees. PAS was a public company and was obligated to make the news public knowledge.

As this development was now official, I wanted to tell my family. First, I shared the news with Ravit, who had obviously been aware of the status of our discussions with PAS. I then told my oldest son, Yigal. This was very good news, and I assumed he would be happy. Therefore, I was surprised to learn he had retreated to his room in tears after my announcement. I went to his room to ask him why he was so sad.

"Daddy," he said through his tears, "all these years you have repeated the story that on January 1992 two children were born to you: the Pepsi business on the sixth and me on the seventh. Now that the business is being sold, what does that mean about my identity?"

I never fully appreciated the profound effect that statement had on my son or how much he identified himself with our operation. I swallowed hard and then explained to him that it was a positive development. The shareholders of the company were going to enjoy a nice return on an investment they held for a long time. It was the right change of ownership for this business from a group of entrepreneurs, who saw the business from inception through growth and relative maturity, to PepsiCo's second largest bottler in the world, with global and regional operations. I explained that it was the best thing that could have happened to the business. The operation may have a new owner, but it would always be very close to my heart.

Yigal seemed to accept my explanation, but his reaction caused me to make an impromptu decision. I was about to travel to Bucharest to meet with PAS's top management and share the news with our employees. I asked Yigal to come with me and be part of the experience.

Two days after official notice was given, I was in Bucharest in front of a packed auditorium of employees. I had carefully crafted a speech, as I knew I would be too excited to improvise. I felt it was very important to deliver the message in the right way. At one point, I asked Yigal to come and stand next to me, and I shared with the audience his reaction to the news and my response to him. Tears streamed down my cheeks, and I could barely finish my speech. It was a joyous moment, but also a very emotional one. Ken Keiser, the COO of PAS, followed me in the presentation. He delivered a very reassuring message to the employees about their commitment to continue our trend of success in the organization. The news was well received, and I left Bucharest feeling satisfied that we had honored our employees with our presentation.

Later that month we held the Tenth Annual Marketing and Sales Conference. Eli had promised the year before that if the company performance continued its upward trend, the tenth conference would be held outside Romania. He made good on his promise, and we flew some three hundred employees to a Club Med resort in Palmiye, near Antalya, Turkey. The resort was beautiful, situated right on the Mediterranean Sea. Club Med typically specialized in sports activities, so we created a series of competitions for the conference and labeled them the Quadrant Olympic Games.

The highlight of the conference was the management presentation in which we shared with our sales force the performance of the company over the previous year. This time we presented the information in the form of a play. The setting was a Turkish harem, and Eli played the role of the sultan. In fact, each of our top managers had a part in the play, complete with appropriate costumes and lines. The atmosphere was truly magical.

A few top PAS managers also attended the event, and one of them took me aside during the activities. He said that when I had given my emotional speech to our employees a couple of weeks earlier, he could not really understand the passion behind my words. Now that he had witnessed the culture of our company firsthand at the conference, he was able to fully appreciate my sentiment.

After the conference, I felt that it was the right moment for another family trip to Romania. This time I invited everyone on my side of the family as well as Ravit's. This operation had been such an important part of my life for so long that I wanted to share it with my entire family before the impending handover to PAS.

Early in June, some twenty family members made the trip. We started in Bucharest, where we visited the usual tourist attractions and, of course, our bottling plant. The plant looked quite different from the first family visit more than ten years earlier. It had transformed into a modern, state-of-the-art bottling facility, and it had hosted delegations from bottlers around the world, including Japan! I was very proud to share this major achievement with my entire family. We also ventured outside of Bucharest and visited the resort town of Poiana Brasov. The trip ended with a lovely lunch that Eli hosted in our honor at his home. It was a wonderful visit for my family and a poignant bit of closure for me.

One final victory would be ours, and it could not have come at a more appropriate time. We were in the midst of the complex closing arrangements with PAS when we received some incredible news. The first quarter Canadean report arrived—a report we had been receiving for years that listed actual sales results for Coke and Pepsi brands. We combed over the numbers in shock. Pepsi sales were higher than Coke! For the first time in our long history, our main brand had outperformed that of our archrival in our market. The ultimate reward for our efforts had at last become a reality.

Our final board meeting under original ownership took place in mid-June in New York. We covered the usual items on the agenda first, such as company performance the previous quarter. Then, we left a fair amount of time for issues related to the transaction with PAS. There was some debate among the board members representing the original group and the representatives of PAS regarding how certain investments made during the previous nine months should be reflected in the purchase price. In the end, a resolution of all issues regarding the final purchase price was left to Alex Ware and me.

The issues took some time to resolve. The mechanism for the price on the balance of the ownership had been set in the agreement of the initial investment made by PAS the previous year, but there were a number of specified adjustments that needed to be settled. We had a number of phone discussions, some involving heated debates. On one phone call, the discussion was particularly intense, and then suddenly the line was cut off. I thought at first that Alex may have hung up on me. A last-minute crisis was all we needed! But Alex called me back within a few minutes and proposed PAS's "final total figure." It was 98 percent of where I wanted to end up. I felt it was close enough and notified our shareholders group. We were finally ready to complete the transaction.

On July 3, 2006, I landed in Bucharest with two of my sons. It was the day of the closing, and I wanted to meet with our top management one last time as the chairman of the company. PAS had asked Eli to stay on as CEO for a transition period, but my role would end with the closing. I had worked with every one of our top managers for a number of years, and had personally appointed a few of them. We had assembled an incredible team, and I knew they would serve the new owners very well. It was good for all of us to assemble one last time for a warm discussion about past victories and future possibilities.

I boarded a plane with my youngest son and left Yigal with Eli to spend a week in Bucharest doing some fieldwork for the company. I felt that it would ease the sale of his "brother" company if he spent some final days involved in the business. The transaction was officially closed. Almost sixteen years after I first heard about the prospect of setting up a beverage business in Romania, we had brought the ship home safely, and this unimaginable journey was complete.

# EPILOGUE

*Someone has well said, "Success is a journey, not a destination." Happiness is to be found along the way, not at the end of the road, for then the journey is over and it is too late. Today, this hour, this minute is the day, the hour, the minute for each of us to sense the fact that life is good, with all of its trials and troubles, and perhaps more interesting because of them.*

**—Robert R. Updegraff**

In the months following the handover of the business to PAS, Eli stayed on to work alongside the newly appointed CEO. He remained involved in all key decisions, so the transfer of power was indeed smooth. Eli also had one more party to organize: he wanted to throw a fitting farewell for me. I had given him a grand party when he left after his first assignment over eleven years earlier, and

Eli wanted to reciprocate. The date was set for late November, and I was invited back to Romania along with Ravit.

I arrived by myself a day early, and our faithful driver, Mihai, was waiting for me at the Bucharest Airport. As we drove toward the hotel, Mihai received a phone call and handed the phone over to me. Someone speaking Romanian fired a number of questions at me. When I explained that I did not speak the language, the anonymous person on the phone switched immediately to English. He told me that he was an officer with the airport police, and I needed to return immediately to the airport. A video camera at the terminal caught my image, and I looked like someone the authorities were looking for. They needed to verify my identity.

I was furious. I told the person on the phone that I had been in charge of a significant company in Romania and had been traveling to and from Bucharest numerous times over the past fifteen years. I had no intention of going back to the airport to prove my identity. He responded angrily that if I did not come back, I would never again be allowed in the country. I paused. Fine, I would return to the airport, but someone was going to pay for this mistake.

"When you return," the person on the phone said, "ask what it means to be on a radio show."

It took but a quick moment for me to realize what was going on. I had been the victim of a joke played by our top management, and they had taped the whole thing for the party the next day!

After my unconventional exit from the airport, I spent the following day visiting our factory and many of the managers. It was the first time since my initial visit in January of 1991 that I had been away from Romania for an extended period. I was once again a visitor, and it was a strange feeling.

In the evening, I was driven to Eli's home for the party. It was a very festive occasion. Eli invited our top management and many other people who had been associated with our business over the years. Ravit arrived just in time to take part in the event. A lovely dinner was served, and then the managers gave a presentation that turned out to be quite a roast at my expense. I laughed through my tears as they made fun of me and gave me some very nice presents. Altogether, it was a wonderful and emotional event. I could not have asked for a better farewell.

The year ended on a very high note. Turnover increased by over 30 percent, approaching $200 million! Profitability also increased by 40 percent. I was pleased that we handed over the business in its best possible financial state.

In early January 2007, we received incredible news: our operation in Romania won PepsiCo's worldwide Bottler of the Year Award! We did it. We landed the top prize in our final year. We were only owners of the business for half of the year, but we were clearly responsible for the results of the entire year, as Eli had remained at the helm through December. In Eli's words, it was "the cherry on top of the cake." We sailed into port at the end of our journey under perfect conditions. It was like a dream.

The new owners did not invite Eli and me to represent the company at PepsiCo International's award ceremony, but it mattered little to me. We knew the prize was ours, and so did everyone else who counted in our minds. Zein and the top management of PI in Europe threw a great dinner party for Eli and me in Geneva shortly after the award ceremony where they officially recognized our efforts.

I suppose this is when we should have sailed off into the sunset, but there are so many new adventures out there. Eli and I started almost immediately to look at a fresh business venture with Pepsi. I had promised my eldest son, Yigal, that I would attempt to continue a relationship with Pepsi, and I intended to honor that promise. Also, both PI and PAS leaned on Eli and me to get involved in a new Pepsi venture. After checking around a bit, we discovered that the neighboring country of Bulgaria held a new opportunity. The bottler there for many years was interested in selling. We looked into acquiring that business and started to travel to Bulgaria to explore the possibilities. By midyear, we reached an agreement with the seller.

We kept the entire group of shareholders from Romania informed about the process and invited them to participate in the new deal. Almost all of them did. In addition, PAS wanted to be a minority shareholder in the new business, which solidified our shareholder group.

In early September, we closed the transaction and became the owners of a new Pepsi operation. It also included the Prigat brand and a local mineral water brand. We were setting sail once again in unexplored waters, but now we were seasoned adventurers.

As we did when we started the business in Romania, we brought on a small team of expatriate managers to bolster the local team. This time they were from...Romania. Among the new managers was Ioan Bucurescu, the person who greeted me on my very first visit to Romania and remained a loyal crew member throughout our involvement there. Antonio was also a key member of our new team, as Bulgaria was part of his territory at PI. He had actually played a big role in our decision to pursue the Pepsi organization in Bulgaria in the first place. In a way, Antonio predicted this when we closed the first part of our transaction with PAS. He wrote to me, "This marks the end of one journey and the beginning of another."

As I put the final touches on this story of our unimaginable journey with Pepsi in Romania, we are more than a year and a half into a new adventure with Pepsi in Bulgaria. The shape of our latest quest is still a mystery. Who will become our passengers and crew members on this voyage? What epic adventures lie ahead? I launch into open waters once again with hope and anticipation. A brilliant sun is peeking over the horizon as we sail on.

www.ingramcontent.com/pod-product-compliance
Lightning Source LLC
Chambersburg PA
CBHW072033190526
45165CB00017B/522